"As I turned fifty-six, the desire to live the life God designed for me has only increased. Living a wild and wonderful life is not just a goal, but my mission now. In Susan's enlightening new book, she encouraged me to refocus on that mission. She asked things like, 'What priority does your life reflect?' Ouch! This can sometimes be a sobering question. As Susan so clearly explains, there is my way and there is God's way, and the choice is ours to make. Through the stories of others and her own personal examples, she makes a case that following Christ is truly the only way to a wild and wonderful life. I know this book will be a blessing to you and everyone you give it to."

Jack Myrick, author of the *Shipbuilder* and *Seeds of Success*

"No one does life quite like Susan. She knows how to throw a jubilee on the beach, she will shed some tears with you through the rains of life, and she somehow creates beautiful memories in the Hospice House. Finding the wonderful in all things wild is how Jesus created her. Wild and wonderful...this is who she is.

Take this book with you on the ride of life for a while. Let these stories and words sink into your everyday thoughts and occurrences. As you journey to the last few pages, you will find Jesus as your constant companion, creating 'wonderful' beauty no matter how crazy the 'wild.' Hear yourself saying along with Susan, *What a wild and wonderful life it is, Jesus!*"

Becky Adam, co-author of *Jumpstart Bible Studies*

"Because we all experience messiness on this journey called life, we need a friendly voice reminding us of the One Hope that can lead us to the other side of our current challenge. You're holding an authentic, friendly voice in your hand. Listen well and hold on tight!

Susan lets you peek in on her journey of trials and triumphs, reminding you why you said *yes!* to Jesus to start with, and how your Jesus story is well on its way to being more than you can imagine! The bumps and bruises of real life bubble up with humor, grace, and cup-of-coffee comfort through Susan's engaging stories of discovering immeasurably more with Jesus on a daily basis."

Dr. Laura Savage-Rains, ministry leader, speaker, founder, and author of *WomensMinistryCoach.com*

"Thankfully, I have a friend in Susan Campbell! She's someone I've leaned on, learned from, listened to and most often laughed with during life's twists and turns. When we meet for coffee, we usually have to apologize for being late to our next appointment! I've driven across town to hear a word from Susan that speaks into a current circumstance; I've also traveled across the world with her to act upon God's Word alongside others.

In writing this book, Susan offers engaging stories and winsome wisdom to show just how wild and wonderful life is with Jesus as a friend. Her words will not only speak straight into your heart, they will enrich your soul with an affirming message of hope for a life full of love, faith, and

friendship. You are made for a wildly wonderful life. It's time to begin living it. Grab your favorite cup of coffee and begin the journey within the pages of this book—just be sure to clear your calendar!"

> **Michelle Funk**, women's ministry program director,
> The United Methodist Church of the Resurrection

"This book proves that life with Jesus is anything but boring. The words are lived out loud every day in Susan's life. She knows the fullness of abundant living with Christ. Daily she takes his outstretched hand on the dance floor, locks eyes with him, and—song-by-song, she follows his lead into wonder-filled adventure. In a generation that is growing increasingly numb to God's majesty, this message charges readers to come back to their first love—the greatest love they will ever know.

Through my calling, I come across people every day who are so hungry for 'something more' but they just don't know that immeasurably more *is* inviting them into the passenger seat of journeying through this life with their Maker. I wish I could give all of them this book. Maybe I will."

> **Morgan Mobley**, KCAU 9 news reporter

"There can be seasons in life when we begin to feel stagnant in our faith and find ourselves wondering, 'Is this the life of faith that I'm meant to live?' Susan has tasted and seen the *wild* and *wonderful* life with Jesus and desires for her readers to experience HIM in a fresh way. Weaving biblical

examples with memorable stories, Susan is living proof of what a wild and wonderful life with Jesus could be. As a Bible study leader and soccer chaplain, I'm constantly in search of resources to offer women that will inspire and challenge them to grown in their faith. This book will definitely be on the list!"

Lori Krueger, volunteer coordinator for chaplains,
National Women's Soccer League
Women's Ministry co-leader, Legacy Christian Church

A WILD & WONDERFUL LIFE

SAY YES TO YOUR IMMEASURABLY MORE JESUS STORY

SUSAN CAMPBELL

More
Than You
Imagine
Ministries

LEAWOOD · KANSAS

A WILD & WONDERFUL LIFE WITH JESUS
Say Yes to Your Immeasurably More Jesus Story
By Susan Campbell

Ministries

More Than You Imagine Publishers
www.morethanyouimagine.org

Unless otherwise indicated, Scripture quotations are from The Holy Bible, New International Version® NIV® Copyright © 1973, 1978, 1984 by International Bible Society

Also used: The New Living Translation (NLT), copyright 1996, 2004, 2015 by Tyndale House Publishers, Inc. Wheaton, Illinois 60189. All rights reserved.

Also Used: The Message, the New Testament in Contemporary English, © 1993 by Eugene H. Peterson, published by NavPress, Colorado Springs, Colorado.

Edited by Susan Tolleson

Cover design: Carly Robinson and Tamara Dever, *TLCGraphics.com*
Interior design: Erin Stark, *TLCGraphics.com*

ISBN: 978-0-9993074-0-3 (softcover)
ISBN: 978-0-9993074-1-0 (e-book)

First Printing 2017

THIS BOOK IS DEDICATED TO...
Jack Bartlett Campbell, the inspiration behind writing my story,
Steven Campbell, the better half of my life story,
Jesus, the one who makes my story better

table of contents

foreword

A Wild and Wonderful Life

When Susan informed me she was writing *A Wild and Wonderful Life*, my first thought was: "Nobody can speak more passionately on this subject than Susan." (If you are skeptical about the wild part, just ask her about her wrist art or trips to Africa).

I have had the pleasure of knowing Susan for all of my twenty-seven years. You see, we are bonded in a unique way. Susan Campbell is my mother.

No one in this world (except for Steve, her husband) is more connected to Susan in such a special way. At least, that's what I would like to believe. I'm a self-proclaimed mama's boy with a heart that has always looked up to my mother. I also have the advantage of being an only child, therefore I didn't have to share with any siblings!

And although I am her son, my bias regarding her qualifications for writing this book are shared by her friends, family, bible study groups, acquaintances, and even cashiers at the grocery store. You get the picture. Susan has chosen to lead a wild and wonderful life that impacts others, to be a guiding light in a world of darkness, and to reveal a purpose for choosing Jesus. And in my humble opinion, she has been tremendously successful.

As a financial analyst, I work with numbers every day. The world we live in seems to want to quantify everything; rank and order all types of activities and dealings. Earthly success often appears to be measured by a dollar amount, bottom line, number of users or followers, material possessions, or raw intelligence. But I wholeheartedly believe Susan's life epitomizes success in the most immeasurable, yet fundamental and essential way: through human relationships.

I have witnessed it over and over. Her unique gift is to not only represent Jesus in her life and relationships, but to bring our Lord and Savior into the room. Countless times I have walked into the house from school or practice or during a holiday and observed her sitting and talking with every type of person—friends, acquaintances, and yes, even some strangers. They may be having coffee, or a Coke® (the real stuff in a glass bottle), nibbling on sorghum cookies, or maybe just chatting, but the presence of Jesus is in that room. It seems as if Jesus is right there at the table or sitting on the couch, nodding his head and listening intently along with Susan. And although she often knows just the right scripture or advice for the tough situations when she doesn't, Susan isn't just hearing... She is really *listening*. As she is putting herself in the other person's shoes, she leaves behind judgment or condemnation, only reflecting the same grace offered by Jesus.

I would be remiss if I didn't mention the passion Susan exudes in her wild and wonderful life. I believe she is divinely called to demonstrate the wonderful nature and fulfillment of a life with Jesus and display the wildness that can come with accepting Jesus in an imperfect world. The way she embraces her Jesus story shows everyone she meets what a wild and wonderful life with Christ can really look like. In fact, I often think about the way Susan has remained a steady leader in her profession—the business of people—over the course of her life. She consistently delivers smiles, prayers, and counsel that lead to life transformations instead of widgets or dollars.

In closing, I am proud to call Susan Campbell my mother, a friend, and the most important spiritual mentor in my life. Many, including myself, have witnessed and/or experienced her incredible influence driven by a spiritual calling deep in her soul. And although we may never be able to quantify the impression she has made on so many in this earthly life, I *know* the Lord has taken notice of her professional success in serving him.

My hope (and I believe it's Susan's hope, as well) for this book is that it blesses you, encourages you, and enlightens you, but most of all, causes you to commit wholeheartedly to a wild and wonderful life with Jesus.

> *What shall we then say to these things?*
> *If God be for us, who can be against us?*
> ROMANS 8:31

Jack Campbell
Son and fan of Susan Campbell

✿ YES ✿

"Do you want to go to Africa?" my friend Debi asked when I bumped into her in the hallway at church.

"Yes, I do."

And that was it. I had no details, no dates, and no purpose for going. Yet I had just committed to traveling to the other side of the world.

I'm not typically a yes person. I tend to say no a lot more. But for some reason, I knew Africa was calling me.

In the months before my friend asked, I had been praying God would open a new door that would take me out of my comfort zone. About to turn fifty, my desire was to do something that added a new purpose to my life. I wanted God to show me how I could do his work in a fresh, new way. Don't get me wrong. I loved what I was doing, but sometimes life needs to be stirred up so we can see things from a different perspective.

I never dreamed God would ask me to go to Malawi, Africa.

My church had been offering trips for a couple of years but honestly, I had never felt the desire or need to go. Now a friend was asking me, and I felt a tug at my heart.

Our team met and planned for our trip. I received my vaccinations, enlisted a prayer partner, and organized my wardrobe for the ten days. When the big day to depart finally came, I was a little anxious about the long flight, but excited to embark on this adventure.

I will always remember landing in Malawi. At the airport arrival gate, hundreds of people eagerly waited to greet their family, friends, and guests. However, near the front of the masses stood four people waving and grinning so big, we could not mistake our hosts. True to the Malawian nickname—"the warm heart of Africa"—these people showed us their warm hearts from the moment we met them.

The days flew by. I don't think I ever learned so much about myself in one trip as I did in Malawi. As I absorbed a new culture, I witnessed love and joy to its fullest. I made friends with people who weren't that much different from me.

And it all happened because a friend asked, and I said yes.

THE POWER OF YES

"Yes" is a powerful word because it draws us into activity. Most things we do begin with a yes or a no. We accept or deny.

* I gladly said yes when my husband asked me to marry him.
* I eagerly said yes when I accepted my first job.
* I cautiously said yes when my neighbor asked me to volunteer at her school.

Sometimes the activity is short-lived and has a beginning and end, like saying yes to having coffee with a friend. But sometimes a yes can dramatically change the course of your life.

There was one particular time when my "yes" changed everything because it was the beginning of my Jesus story. I said yes to Jesus when I was nine years old. I prayed and asked him to become part of my life. My parents told me Jesus now lived in my heart. At the time, I wasn't exactly sure what it meant for someone to live in a heart. But I did know Jesus made a lot of great promises and I really liked that.

For me, the most meaningful promise Jesus made was this: "I will never leave you or let you be alone" (Hebrews 13:5, NLV). Even at nine, I loved the idea that someone would be with me always like a friend. And since then, Jesus has been my constant companion.

When I was fourteen years old, we moved to a new town, and I felt like no one wanted to be my friend. But Jesus was there. My first high school breakup left me feeling worthless, but Jesus valued me. He reminded me I wasn't a loser when I made my first failing grade in college (perhaps he just simply nudged me to study more).

Through the years, I have moved all over the country, and he's been with me. He's comforted me when I was sad about leaving friends and feeling alone. He understood when I felt hurt by disappointments, loss of dreams, and failures. He rejoiced at my wedding and the birth of my son.

Saying yes to Jesus is the beginning of a wild and wonderful life. Although Jesus doesn't use the exact words "wild and wonderful," he does make a lot of promises about what a life with him might look like.

Let me give you an example. I love gardens—flower gardens, in particular. During growing season, I spend time working in my garden. Mostly, I pull weeds, trim scraggly plants, and deadhead flowers. When I'm not so regular at tending to my flowers, weeds easily grow among them. It can get a little wild looking. And regardless if there are weeds or not, when my garden is in full bloom, there are so many varieties of flowers that, to some, my garden may look a little wild and even perhaps unruly. Either way, wildly weedy or wildly flowery, it's still my wonderful garden.

Throughout the season, I will clip flowers so I have fresh ones in my home at all times. When friends stop by, they usually comment on my flowers. Many times the word "wonderful" is used to describe them.

The thing is, when my friends look at the flowers on my table, they are not able to discern if those flowers came from the wild, weedy garden that I neglected for a few days or if they came from the wild masses in my well-tended garden. This is what a wild and wonderful life with Jesus is like. Wildly good or wildly hard, when Jesus joins your story, the end result is wonderful.

Maybe your life is feeling a little unwound, unknown, crazy, or even stagnant—like an untended garden. It's okay. Jesus is a master gardener. He is not afraid of your mess. He can handle your doubts and fears. More than anything, he wants to join in all your endeavors, walk alongside you every day, and even prune a few of your weeds so that the two of you become partners in every part of your life story.

Jesus wants to do your wild and wonderful
journey together.

All you have to do is say YES.

Before you begin, there are three facts about *yes* you need
to know.

The first fact:
God said yes to you first.

God said yes to you before you even began to think about
saying yes to him. See what the Bible says:

> *Whatever God has promised gets stamped with the Yes*
> *of Jesus. In him, this is what we preach and pray,*
> *the great Amen, God's Yes and our Yes together,*
> *gloriously evident. God affirms us, making us a sure thing*
> *in Christ, putting his Yes within us.*
> 2 CORINTHIANS 1:20-21, THE MESSAGE

There are more than 5,000 promises in the Bible. God promised and Jesus said yes to every one of them for you. Jesus is
the yes that makes every promise possible. All 5,000 of them.

Needing some comfort? **Jesus.**
Desiring peace? **Jesus.**
Feeling a little hopeless? **Jesus.**
Grateful today? **Jesus.**
Wanting to sing because you feel blessed? **Jesus.**

So, even before you were born, every one of God's promises
was a gift for your wild and wonderful life.

The second fact:

There is one "yes" more important than all the others.

You will have many opportunities to say yes in your lifetime. You will say yes to both small and grand choices. But there is one yes that far outweighs any other. It is when you say yes to Jesus. Saying yes to him is the beginning of your Jesus story. And because Jesus takes center stage in your story, it promises to be immeasurably more than you imagine.

The third fact:

God's yes and your yes combined
is what makes life wild and wonderful.

* Maybe you have never known Jesus but are hopeful life can be richer than what you are experiencing now.

* Maybe you are just beginning your journey with Jesus and don't really know what it's all about.

* Maybe you have known Jesus for awhile now but feel your faith is stagnant and wonder if there is more to life than just going through the motions.

* Maybe you're busy, so Jesus sometimes gets placed on the back burner, but you want nothing more than to put him front and center in your life.

If any of these are true for you, then I wrote this book for you.

I'm wondering if you sometimes:

* feel alone even though people are all around you
* ask yourself, "who am I?"

* desire God's promises to be true in your life but feel they are unattainable
* wish faith was more simple
* feel hopeless and wonder if God is even there
* sense God loves you but have never really experienced it fully
* long to live your life well

If so, I want you to know Jesus is willing to establish himself wherever you are in your life. Your yes joined with Jesus is the launching pad for a wild and wonderful life.

This book uses real stories to describe a life with Jesus. You will learn how life involves baby steps, skipping steps, giant steps, and sometimes even a few steps backwards. It's a life where setbacks can be turned into opportunities. It's a life where Jesus gives direction about what matters along the way. So if you're wondering where Jesus fits into your story, please join me.

Each chapter uses a word to describe what a wild and wonderful life with Jesus might look like.

FRIENDSHIP

Jesus wants to be your friend. He doesn't want to be simply an acquaintance you run into at the grocery store. Instead, he longs to be a lifelong friend who knows you well and still likes you a lot! Saying yes to a friendship with Jesus means you have a constant companion.

TRANSFORMATION

Not only does Jesus want to become your best friend, he also wants to help you become your best you. Jesus knows the answer to your question, "who am I?" He sees you, not for who you are, but who you can become. He sees things you cannot see in yourself. When you are confused about life's choices, Jesus reminds you what is important and gives your life direction. He helps you identify the things that matter most. When you allow Jesus to transform you, you begin to become the best version of you.

LOVE

The most basic fact about God is that he is love. How much does he love you? He would give his most valuable possession for you (and he has). He would move heaven and earth for you. He delights in you. You are the apple of his eye. You are the one he claims as his child. You are cherished. Your God is the Heavenly Father who loves you lavishly and extravagantly. These are the amazing facts about God's love for you. Accepting God's love helps you understand how valued and important you are to him.

LIFE

Maybe you struggle with reading the Bible because the ideas and words seem confusing and you wrestle with the tough parts. Perhaps you don't know where to start. Don't give up—there are numerous resources to help you. And even though the Bible may seem like a dusty old history book, it's actually alive and active. When you open your Bible, you begin an exciting journey where history is replaced with hope. Reading it can give you a new perspective, encourage you where you never thought possible, and teach you more about God and his wonderful ways. Once you start reading it, you learn more about God's promises and begin to imagine the life he wants for you. No other book is packed with so much wisdom—it is practical and relevant while demonstrating love and teaching life's truths.

CHILDLIKE FAITH

Even though you want your faith to be solid and mature, Jesus says your faith should actually be like that of a child. Think how children's faces light up the first time they see snow or how they take to a new bike with reckless abandon. A wild and wonderful life with Jesus resembles a childlike faith where amazement and enthusiasm are a part of everyday adventures. This may be as simple as taking a moment to stop and notice something great God has done. Or perhaps it means calling out to God when you face a fear and then watching him work things out. Practicing childlike faith will teach you to count your blessings, face your fears, pursue what you love, and trust God more.

HOPE

Do you wonder if God is there when you struggle with difficult things? When life brings obstacles that detour your perfect plans, do you question if God really cares? The Bible does not say *if* you have troubles, it says *when* you have troubles. Troubles will indeed come, but Jesus says that he has overcome the world. This may seem difficult to grasp when you are in the middle of something hard. But hope is the great reminder that even in the middle of your difficult circumstances, God loves you and will never leave you alone in your situation.

WHOLEHEARTED

Your life is not a short story. A wholehearted life is the accumulation of your life experiences masterfully woven together by God. Some days you feel like you have the world on a string. It feels like nothing can go wrong. Other days, you strive to just get by. It's a challenge to do everything well all the time. But God's desire is for you to constantly remember his faithfulness so you can follow him better and trust his promises in your circumstances.

ANOTHER TIME I SAID YES

Not too long ago, I said another yes to God. It was a big yes. I said yes to writing this book. By doing so, I stepped out of my comfort zone. This has not been a natural journey for me. Writing a book is hard. Sharing personal stories is scary. Wondering if anyone will read it is daunting.

But here it is. Because I said yes.

I hope you won't judge me too harshly. I pray you will be my cheerleader instead and say, "She did it! She said yes!"

Saying yes is sometimes risky. It can involve the unknown. But saying yes can be the greatest experience of your life. I'm praying you will say yes:

* Yes to reading this book.
* Yes to experiencing the abundant life Jesus promises.
* Yes to a myriad of opportunities you've been hesitant to take.
* Yes to asking Jesus to join you on your journey.

In the pages ahead, you will read about people who lived imperfect lives—mine included. The common thread is they all said yes to Jesus.

If you choose to say yes, there is no guarantee everything will turn out exactly as you planned. And I can't promise that you won't experience difficult times along the way. However, saying yes to Jesus means he is with you every step of your journey. You won't be alone as you travel.

And this is what makes life both wild and wonderful.

You might say, "wild doesn't sound so great." Well then, perhaps you are only looking at part of what the word "wild" means. Sure, it can mean to be hard, crazy, and out of control. But wild doesn't have to define only the difficult things in life. It can also mean to be exciting and passionate.

Your life encompasses it all—the wildly good and the wildly hard. And through it all, Jesus promises to be with you.

That's pretty wonderful.

chapter one

✿ FRIENDSHIP ✿

Do You Like Peas?

I have called you friends.
JOHN 15:15

Immeasurably more means Jesus calls you his best friend.

THE WOMAN WITH NO FRIENDS IN JOHN 4

She awoke in the same way as most mornings—worn out. The night before had not been good to her. Every bone in her body ached, and her head felt like it was about to explode. With two feet on the ground, she hoisted her tired body off the bed. She pulled on the nearest garment, slipped on her sandals, and grabbed her water jug. She must get to the well and retrieve water so she can drink her first cup of coffee.

What time was it anyway? The sun was straight up in the sky indicating it was about noon. All the other women in the town would have been to the well earlier in the morning. They were friends with each other. She was the outcast.

1

Expecting nothing except to fill her jug, the woman walked alone to the center of town to fetch her water.

She was surprised to see a man sitting at the well. It was a man named Jesus. They sat for awhile in silence, but finally he asked, "Will you give me a drink?" (John 4:7) The conversation began. The two sat and talked. Knowing this woman's needs were much greater than just for water from the well, Jesus made an incredible promise to her. He told her that if she would drink the water he gave, she would never thirst again.

He went on to say his water would become like a spring of water welling up to eternal life. That sounded pretty great to a woman who was tired, worn out, and broken— to a woman whose life had not turned out exactly as she had expected. She said yes to his living water, and their friendship began.

As the two talked, she realized she liked Jesus. He appeared to be genuine. She could trust him. He spoke words she could understand and believe. She said, "I know that Messiah is coming. When he comes, he will explain everything to us" (John 4:25). She secretly wished this man was the Messiah. Then Jesus told her what she had hoped: "I who speak to you am he" (John 4:26).

Wild, isn't it? She went to the well looking for some water and instead found the Living Water.

DO YOU LIKE PEAS?

My mom always called the period of time when people are becoming friends the "do you like peas" stage. This is when you are learning about each other's likes, dislikes, and backgrounds. Spending time in the "do you like peas" stage helps move relationships from just an acquaintance to a friendship. This is what happened with Gina and me.

Gina is my best friend. We didn't begin our friendship knowing everything about each other; it took time and experiences. We met through our kids' school. Both of our families were new to the area.

One day shortly after the school year started, we ran into each other at a store. Gina recognized me as the mother of the new boy. She approached me. We immediately connected and scheduled a walking date. After our long and chatty walk the next day, Gina came to my house, and we visited for three more hours! Both of us longed for a friend. We were ready to move past the "do you like peas" stage and really get to know each other.

Jesus also used "do you like peas" with the woman at the well. He started by asking her for a drink of water. Today, this would be like asking someone about the weather. He used ordinary and normal things to get to know the woman. Somewhere along the line, the two moved past introductions and became friends. Even though the woman had no idea she was about to make a new friend, her willingness to believe Jesus and his words made them more than acquaintances. In fact, when Jesus was on earth, he gladly spent time with people who had no friends. He was—and is—most open to those who are willing to hear his words and respond.

In John 15:15, Jesus says, "I have called you friends." In this passage, he is speaking to his disciples. They have spent three intimate years together. During this time, they've eaten together, labored together, and celebrated together. The disciples have learned from Jesus. They have questioned him, challenged him, and even doubted him. Yet, Jesus calls each of them his friends.

I think these might be five of the most significant words in the Bible because Jesus says them—not just to his disciples—but as a direct invitation to each and every one of us. He's not talking about a generic friendship, but a one-on-one relationship designed just for you and him. Each of us must decide if Jesus' invitation to be his personal friend is what we want. When I was nine years old, I decided it was and allowed these five little words to change my life forever.

When I made my decision, my relationship with Jesus was much like the "do you like peas" stage. I didn't immediately know everything about him the day we became friends. I attended church and learned simple things about him. My Sunday school teachers and parents read the Bible to me and taught me short Bible verses. And as our relationship grew, I wanted to know him better.

Jesus calls you friend, too. Just like a relationship with a girlfriend, your friendship with Jesus begins at the "do you like peas" stage and develops from there. For some reason, we often compare our friendship with Jesus to other women. We think there are better pray-ers, smarter Bible study students, and wiser women than us. However, your relationship with Jesus is uniquely yours, and your level of friendship is not about where someone else is spiritually. Jesus wants your friendship to grow in the way that is best for you.

FRIENDS MAKE HISTORY
BY DOING STUFF TOGETHER

Gina and I have known each other for many years. But we weren't always best buddies. Over the years, we have done all kinds of crazy stuff together:

* Changed our hair color numerous times.

* Performed every workout program available on the market.

* Shopped for any beauty product known to humankind.

* Tried every Mexican restaurant in Kansas City.

* Walked hundreds of miles while solving world problems (and girl problems).

* Gained weight *and* lost weight.

* Traveled together and stayed home together (when the power was out).

* Laughed, cried, been silent, and talked... a lot.

Of course, this isn't a comprehensive list. It would take years to name all the fun (and not-so-fun) things we've done together. But at this point in our lives, if you can name it, we've pretty much done it.

Gina and I have a tradition for practically everything. For birthdays, we celebrate hers over lunch with a mini strawberry or white cake (Gina has a hard time deciding) from McLain's Bakery. We celebrate my birthday over breakfast — also with a mini, but always white, cake from McLain's.

When our kids were still in school, we took a short trip on the last day of school. We made Christmas cookies together. We visited the local pumpkin patch in the fall. We toured remodeled homes for the school fundraiser. We attended the annual holiday craft show. We just liked spending time with each other.

A few years ago, we spent much of our time together dealing with more difficult circumstances. One morning, I called Gina. My father and I were in the emergency room. He was failing. Although my sweet and wonderful husband was on his way, I still needed my friend. While we waited for my husband to arrive, Gina sat with me as I read Bible verses to my father.

Three weeks later, I was in a meeting at church when I received a call from the nursing home where my mother was staying. The nurse told me she was failing fast and I needed to hurry over. When I arrived, the nurse met me at the door and said my mother would probably not last the day. I called my brother and sister with the sad news.

But before I made the next call, I realized my phone was just about out of power. My fingers automatically dialed Gina. Without hesitation, she brought my charger to me. This small act may seem insignificant, but knowing Gina would not only answer my phone call, but drop anything she was doing to help me was huge. When she walked in the room, charger in hand, I was beyond grateful. But more, I was so glad to see her face and feel her loving arms around me.

The thing is, neither of us would trade any of our experiences because doing life together has been rich. We have lived through happy times, stressful times, sad times, and challenging times. But along the way, it has been special to experience the things of life with a friend. Simply put, we have made a history that began the day we met and continues today.

HOW THE WOMAN WITH NO FRIENDS CHANGED HER HISTORY

So far in life, her history hasn't been worth remembering. She certainly wasn't proud of it. In fact, she preferred to forget it. Jesus knew everything about her past. During their conversation, he reminded her that she had had five husbands and the one she was living with wasn't even her husband. But Jesus didn't care about her past. And as the friendship progressed, it became apparent he was more interested in her future. She believed Jesus and his words and her new life began.

After her first meeting with Jesus at the well, she returned to town, leaving the very thing she went to get—her water. With Jesus as her friend, she could leave her past behind and look towards the future with hope. For her, new life began at the well.

In town, she exclaimed, "He told me everything I ever did" (John 4:39). Shamed no longer, this woman had been given a new life and new history. Her life was an open book to Jesus, but he loved her anyway. No longer did her past matter. Her history was just that—history. She was ready to begin writing her Jesus story with her new best friend that she had met at the well.

YOUR HISTORY BEGINS WITH JESUS

Your history with Jesus begins the day you say yes to becoming his friend. No matter where you are in your life's journey, it's never too late to begin making a new history with Jesus.

A friendship with Jesus can be like a relationship with your best friend, only better. In many ways, my friendship with Jesus is kind of like my relationship with Gina. We started out as acquaintances then became friends.

Maybe you never thought about Jesus as your friend. Perhaps you have always placed him in heaven but not in your heart. But if you think about it, that's where our friends live—in our hearts. Even if I'm not physically with my friends every minute of the day, I still consider them my friends.

For example, I was out of town the day Gina's mother passed away. My heart was incredibly sad for my friend, but my body was more than 1700 miles away from her. That distance didn't lessen my feelings or hurt for her. I was still holding my grieving friend in my heart.

The same is true with Jesus. You may not feel his physical presence every minute of the day, but you can still know he is present in your heart. Ephesians 3:17 says, "...so that Christ may dwell in your hearts through faith."

So how do you make Jesus your best friend? You do the same type of things you would do with your earthly best friend. You get to know him. You spend more time with him. You work on your relationship, even when it's difficult. For me, it has taken time, experiences, and genuine love for Jesus and me to become the friends we are today. And even though we are past the "do you like peas" stage, there is still plenty of room to grow in our friendship.

One thing I do to continually cultivate my friendship with Jesus is memorize Bible verses about him. These verses are promises that help me in my daily life. For example, I've learned that Jesus is the light of the world and because of this, I don't have to walk in darkness anymore (John 8:12). I've embraced his claim of good shepherd and know he is willing to lay down his life for me (John 10:11). I've realized he is my wonderful counselor who guides me in all wisdom (Isaiah 9:6). I've trusted that he is the image of an invisible God and because of this, I can know what God is like (Colossians 1:15).

One night, I was leading a Bible study for a group of high school girls in my home. I asked the girls to name their favorite miracle Jesus performed in the Bible. As we went around the group, they shared one by one. When we got to the last gal in the group, who was very new to Bible study, she responded timidly, "I don't know any miracles that Jesus performed." My heart broke because I realized how insensitive I had been to ask this question when there were participants in the group who might not have known scripture.

I got up off the floor and moved to where she sat in the circle, put my arms around her and said, "Every one of us started our friendship with Jesus not knowing about his miracles. We all must get to know Jesus in our own way and in our own time." I was so proud of this young lady because she came back to my home each week wanting to learn more about Jesus. Her journey was her own and I loved watching as her Jesus story moved past the "do you like peas" stage.

With Jesus, your past doesn't matter because he's interested in making a new history with you. Your friendship doesn't stop when you say yes to Jesus. It progresses from the "do you like peas" stage to a deep, long-lasting friendship. Being friends with Jesus means you have someone to ride alongside you on the roller coaster called life. You have a partner on the ups and downs, the highs and lows, and the bumps and obstacles.

Simply put, Jesus becomes a partner in your story. Life may still be wild—wildly good or wildly crazy—but a friendship with Jesus helps make it wonderful.

FRIENDS CREATE A SENSE OF HOME

Home is the feeling you get when you smell fresh-baked banana bread wafting from the oven, or when you stay in your pajamas on a rainy day and read a book or watch *I Love Lucy* reruns. Home is your favorite outfit and comfy shoes. Home is where you are comfortable.

One reason I like doing things with Gina is because I am comfortable around her. I would even say Gina gives me a sense of home. For example, one night we were taking a walk, laughing at ourselves as we talked about all the stupid things we worried about that turned out okay. I loved that time with my friend because she allowed me to share almost anything without holding it against me.

Not only does Gina give me a sense of home, she also gets me. For example, when my son called in the middle of an outing, Gina wasn't bugged that I talked with him for more than 20 minutes. "You just take the call from your kid, no matter where you are," she said. I love her for that. When I'm spending time with Gina, I can be myself. She knows me best and still likes hanging out with me.

My husband and I moved to another house after our son left for college. I worried when he returned home on breaks, the new house wouldn't feel like his home. Many of his childhood memories were attached to our former house. Sure, we set up a room for him in the new house and placed all his stuff in there, but would it be the same?

A year or so after we moved, we picked up our son from the airport during a break. I will never forget his comment as we walked in the back door: "It just always feels and smells like home when I walk through this door." I realized that for my son, home wasn't just a physical place. It was more about the people who lived there and the peace he experienced in that place. For him, home was the love of his mom and dad, the tranquility of his purring cat, and the yummy dinner he was about to eat with his family. Home was where he experienced love, felt secure and sensed peace.

JESUS GIVES A SENSE OF HOME

Living with six different men certainly didn't give her a sense of home. It had been a long time, if ever, since she felt comfortable around someone. But there was just something different about Jesus. He knew her faults and loved her anyway.

He spent time with her when no one else would. He spoke to her while others kept to themselves. He saw the woman for what she could become, not what she had been. So it was only natural that after they became friends, she asked

Jesus to spend some more time in her town. Jesus under-stood the importance of spending time together, so he stayed two more days.

Eventually, Jesus left. But the woman at the well would stay close to him because now, like a friend, he lived in her heart. She had never before experienced the peace and secu-rity Jesus offered.

When she became friends with Jesus, her struggles did not automatically go away. But her perspective changed. Jesus showed the woman that she was valued by him. He demonstrated genuine care and concern. Life was still going to be wild. But for this woman, a friendship with Jesus was like going home.

We, also, can experience a sense of home with Jesus by accepting his love, even if we don't feel very lovely. We can trust him on this because he says, "I have loved you just as my Father has loved me" (John 15:9, NLV). We can also feel his comfort and peace by spending more time with him in prayer and reading the Bible. The more of our heart we give him, the bigger presence he establishes. And one day, we realize our friendship with Jesus feels just like home.

GOOD FRIENDSHIPS INVOLVE EFFORT

Certainly, Gina and I experienced our ups and downs over the years. Sustaining a friendship isn't automatic. Our bond has taken time and effort. As with any friendship, sometimes I do not feel like making an effort. To be perfectly honest, being friends with someone is not always the easiest thing to do. Occasionally, priorities are different, or conflicting agendas get in the way. There are a variety of reasons why friendships suffer.

Once our kids graduated from high school, it eliminated one of the common denominators for Gina and me. Whereas, keeping in touch used to come naturally, Gina and I must now carve out time to see each other. There was a period when I was working a lot of hours and was too distracted to be a very good friend. During that time, our friendship suffered. Gina would call, but I was rarely available. Fortunately, we have moved past that season. Today, it still takes effort to see each other, but it's totally worth it because our friendship is important to us.

I love Gina and can't imagine life without her. She and I have gone from the "do you like peas" stage to sharing our deepest thoughts, our everyday lives, and our hopes and dreams. My friendship with Gina reminds me why God gave us earthly friendships. He wants us to know how important relationships are to him. He also wants us to know our earthly friendships can look a lot like our friendship with him.

There can be times in your life when it is more difficult to pursue your friendship with Jesus. Busy schedules, lack of commitment, or dry seasons can prevent you from growing and sustaining your friendship with him. Realizing this is important.

During these times, recognize that greater effort on your part might be necessary. Perhaps you will need to carve out a new time in your schedule to meet with him. You could do something like I did a couple of years ago. I set my phone alarm to noon everyday. When my phone rang, my screen showed it was Jesus calling. I always took the call and usually I would tell whoever I was with to "excuse me while I get this call from Jesus." It turned out to be a fun, new way to focus on him during the middle of my day.

Maybe you will pursue him in different places. Instead of the comfortable chair at home, you might meet him in your car while waiting in the pickup line at the school. Or maybe you make a special time in your schedule and meet him at a coffee shop where you spend a few minutes journaling or reading your Bible. Your friendship with Jesus is important even during the dry spells. Keep at it. It's totally worth your effort.

JESUS IS MY BEST FRIEND

It's been more than 40 years since Jesus became my friend. Together, we have experienced the ups and downs of life. Many years ago, my husband, son, and I were living in Houston. We had recently moved from a city where we had lots of friends. I remember a particularly quiet day. My son was at school and my husband was at work. It was just me. With no friends yet in our new town, I felt very alone.

That morning, I had been reading the Psalms, which speak so much of God's enduring love and presence. Later in the day, still feeling melancholy, I sat on the stairs overlooking my backyard patio. Sitting there quietly, I heard a soft voice. It was the voice of the friend I had known since I was nine. It was Jesus reminding me I was never alone, and that he was *always* with me, living in my heart. It was like a drink of fresh water.

And I remembered what he told the woman at the well, the woman who had no friends. He said that if she would drink his water, she would never thirst again. In that moment, I realized I was not friendless. I had the best friend a person could *ever* have. His name was Jesus.

A FINAL THOUGHT ABOUT THE WOMAN WITH NO FRIENDS

Years ago, when I read the story of the woman at the well, I wondered why she didn't have a name. Many, if not most, of the accounts in Scripture give people's names. Why not her? Although I can't be sure, I think I know why. I believe this woman really lived and met Jesus. But I also believe she is representative of all people. You are the woman at the well. I am the woman at the well. Every one of us is being asked if we are willing to partake of living water—of Jesus.

Like the woman at the well, each one of us must decide if we are willing to say yes to Jesus. If we do, our friendship begins with the "do you like peas" stage. Then it transitions from just acquaintances to a deeper relationship because we get to know him better. As we spend time together, our friendship grows. Over time, we realize how much Jesus loves us and how comfortable he makes us feel.

Wild, isn't it? These five simple words, "I have called you friends," become a game-changer. Jesus *chooses* to be your best friend.

IMMEASURABLY MORE MEANS

✳ It takes a lifetime to get to know Jesus.

✳ Spending time with Jesus makes life more meaningful.

✳ Your relationship with Jesus may not always come automatically. Like any relationship, it takes work and time.

YOUR JESUS STORY

✳ What are some things you can do to get to know Jesus better?

✳ Think about creating a special place to worship or a special time you spend with Jesus each day.

✳ What kinds of things do you think of when you hear the word *home*? How can this sense of home make Jesus real to you?

My dear friend Jesus,

I am simply amazed that you call me friend because sometimes I don't act like a very good friend to you. I disappoint you, let you down, and neglect you. Yet, you still want a relationship with me. You bring me joy, which you say brings YOU joy. That's the kind of friend you are, Jesus. One who loves so much that you would give up literally everything for me—including your life—so I may experience your love and your joy.

Amen.

chapter two

TRANSFORMATION

Bad Photos in a Graduation Scrapbook

And we, who with unveiled faces all reflect the Lord's glory,
are being transformed into his likeness with ever-increasing
glory, which comes from the Lord, who is the Spirit.
2 CORINTHIANS 3:18

**Immeasurably more means
Jesus transforms you into
the best version of you.**

After an unsuccessful afternoon of wedding dress shopping with my future mother-in-law, we stopped at the grocery store to pick up a few items for dinner. I was disappointed that I hadn't seen my dream dress that day.

As we stood in the checkout line, I picked up the recent issue of a bridal magazine. On the cover was the most beautiful wedding dress I'd ever seen. In a pouty voice, I commented to my mother-in-law, "This is the exact dress I would love to wear on my wedding day. I'm sure it costs a million dollars!" Calmly and matter-of-factly, my mother-in-law said, "I can

19

make that dress for you." I knew my mother-in-law was an excellent seamstress, but in my wildest dreams I never imagined she could make my wedding dress!

Fast forward to our wedding day. The beautiful dress was hanging in the bridal dressing room at the church. My hair and makeup were complete, so it was now time to put on the lovely dress. Ready, I walked to the back of the church and saw 300 friends and family standing and looking at me. A little sweat broke out on my forehead and upper lip. Seeing all those people staring at me made me nervous. So I looked at the man at the end of the aisle who was beaming at me; my future husband. I wondered when he looked back at me, which do you think he saw: a nervous young girl or a glowing bride in a beautiful white dress?

My identity was about to change forever from girlfriend to wife. That day, I became a wife, not because of what I was wearing and not because of how I looked. Becoming a wife involved the simple act of a woman saying yes to a man and beginning their journey together. A transformation took place. From that point on, I was Steve's wife.

We've been married more than thirty years, and I have learned a lot. When we married, I wasn't a very good cook, didn't do the laundry well, and lacked certain skills on living with another person. Today, I am certainly far from perfect, but through years of experience and practice, I would like to think I have improved in my role as wife.

One of the great questions in life is "Who am I?" This is also one of the most challenging questions. The good news is that God knows who we are. He has the ability to see us not only as we are today, but also for whom we can become tomorrow. Because of this, perhaps we should ask a better question: "God, who do you want me to become?" When we ask this question, we are asking God to show us how we can become the best version of ourselves. When we do this, true transformation begins.

MY GRADUATION SCRAPBOOK

When I graduated from high school, my mother gave me a scrapbook that chronicled my life from birth to eighteen years. I enjoyed looking at the photos and seeing my life as it had progressed to that point. If you think about it, a person changes substantially from birth to eighteen. For example, we get teeth, we lose teeth, and then get more teeth. Our face begins with soft, blemish-free baby skin, which then becomes bumpy teenager acne-prone skin. Our feet grow, as does every other part of our body. We change a lot, and those are just some of the obvious physical ones.

During my pre-teen years, my legs grew disproportionately compared to the rest of my body. They were so long that I sort of looked like I was standing on stilts. Pants were never long enough. (I was reminded of this as I thumbed through the scrapbook!) For some reason, my mother decided to include one particular photo of me standing pigeon-toed in awful brown shoes wearing red, white, and blue-striped bell-bottom, too-short jeans and a white peasant top (which is back in style). It's an image I would prefer to forget. My friend Martha says there are no bad photos of our children because we just press the delete button on the camera or phone and take another picture. How I wish my mother would have pressed the delete button on this photo!

Thankfully, the Bible promises life with Jesus involves transformation for each of us. Second Corinthians 3:18 says, "…we reflect the Lord and are transformed into His likeness." How I wished someone would have told me this when I was younger. Even though it may have been hard to believe, it sure would have been a confidence booster when I was wearing those striped jeans.

IF GIDEON HAD HAD A SCRAPBOOK

There are no photos of people in the Old Testament. However, if there were, it would be interesting to see a picture of Gideon. He was one of the Old Testament judges and a true Bible nerd. The Bible doesn't give us a lot of information about what he looked like, but we have clues.

Here's how I think Gideon might have looked in his high school scrapbook: He is a short man weighing 120 pounds—soaking wet. He has bucked teeth and acne. He wears two-inch-thick black-rimmed glasses. His pants are pulled tight around his skinny waist, causing his too-long belt to dangle. His white tube socks are always visible because his pants are too short. In other words, if Gideon had a scrapbook, this would be a photo he would have wanted deleted.

Not only was Gideon challenged from a physical perspective, he also came from the wrong side of the tracks. The Bible says, "Gideon's clan was the weakest and Gideon was the least in his father's house" (Judges 6:15). His family was poor, and he was from the smallest tribe of Israel. No one believed Gideon would ever amount to much. However, God saw something in Gideon that others could not see.

Christians get a bad rap. Some people think we are weird. But it seems when God wants to do big things for his kingdom and his people, he prefers to use nerds. The Bible is filled with stories of people who were under-equipped, small, handicapped in some way, insecure, and/or homeless. Perhaps one of the reasons God chooses to use the least and the small is so others can see his great works performed through them.

When God came across that awful photo in my graduation scrapbook, I wonder if he saw the same potential in me that he saw in Gideon?

THE CLOSET EXPERIENCE

I was thirty years old, with a toddler, living in a new town. My life seemed very unsettled. I had always planned to be a working woman. And now, with the latest transfer of my husband's job, I found I was unemployed once again. This was a bummer because I liked working. I identified myself as a working woman.

I will never forget the day I had a "closet" experience. By closet, I mean the place where I kept my clothes. Walking into my small closet, I encountered the age-old problem every woman has experienced at one time or another in her life—I had nothing to wear.

For me, this was a little more than true. More than half of my closet consisted of suits and skirts; clothing I wore when I was employed. On this day, I was in desperate need of sweats and a grungy t-shirt, something I didn't mind getting a little dirty while hanging out with a two-year old.

As I looked around the closet, a great sadness came over me. I realized my life did not represent the clothes in my closet. "Who was I?" I wondered. I certainly wasn't the woman who put on a suit, pumps, and pantyhose. And yet, I didn't feel like I belonged in sweats, either. It was confusing because I didn't know where I belonged in my own world.

For years I had known God. But now, I was curious how he saw *me*. In that closet, I cried out to God and asked him to show me the woman he wanted me to become. Little did I know, but a transformation was about to begin.

ISRAEL CRIES OUT TO GOD

In the Bible, Israel is called God's chosen people although many times they did not act the part. Judges 6 begins this way: "Again, the Israelites did evil in the eyes of the Lord and for seven years he gave them into the hands of the Midianites" (verse 1).

Because the Midianites were so mean and scary, many of the Israelites had moved to mountain clefts and caves. Whenever the Israelites planted their crops, the Midianites invaded their country. Israel was scared, exhausted, and hungry. In desperation, the Israelites cried out to God.

God answered them. He enlisted Gideon, the nerdy guy, to go and save Israel from Midian, the big bully and evil enemy. He even called Gideon by a name that no one else would ever think to use for him. God named Gideon *mighty warrior* in Judges 6:12. It seems God thought nerdy was acceptable.

It is important to note that God called Gideon a mighty warrior—not because Gideon *was* a mighty warrior or because Gideon *believed* he was a mighty warrior—but because Gideon was about to become one. Unlike everyone else, God did not look at Gideon's limited abilities. Instead, God saw all the possibilities.

Many years ago, a movie premiered called *Oh God*. George Burns plays God, who comes to visit Jerry, an assistant grocery store manager (played by John Denver) and asks him to spread his message to the world. Jerry is reluctant at first, but God (George Burns) is persistent. Eventually, after many trials and tests, Jerry agrees.

This movie is not far off from the opening scene in the story of Gideon. God asked Gideon to save Israel from the hand of Midian. But Gideon is very reluctant to serve. He reminds the Lord that "his clan is the weakest in Manasseh and that he is the least in his family" (Judges 6:15). God gives Gideon great confidence: "I will be with you, and you will strike down all the Midianites" (Judges 6:16).

Can you imagine that? God is telling Gideon that, together, they will conquer the nation that has been bullying his people for seven years. Like Jerry in *Oh God*, Gideon asks God (the real one, not George Burns) for a sign to show that he really was God. In a miraculous moment, fire consumes the meat Gideon offered to God, and he realized God was really God. Immediately, Gideon builds an altar to God to worship him.

THE KITCHEN TABLE EXPERIENCE

Soon after the closet experience, something else happened that I call the "kitchen table" experience. The closet experience had prompted me to ask God to reveal the kind of person he wanted me to become. I was also tired of not knowing my place, so I sought God. Like Gideon, I asked him to give me a sign. He did.

God spoke to me while I was sitting at my kitchen table one day. It sounds kind of mysterious, but it wasn't. I asked him out loud: "God, what do you want me to be?" And I heard his voice as if he were sitting next to me.

I don't know how I heard his voice. But I am certain God spoke to me, and I heard his voice. It might have been audible or it may have been a voice in my head. But, no doubt, God spoke. And when he did, he told me to do the oddest thing. He instructed me to create and implement a women's ministry program at my church.

"You want me to lead a bunch of women at my church?" I asked. "Surely not. I don't even like women very much." (God is smiling.) For weeks, I had been asking God to show me a direction in my life, and when he miraculously spoke, instead of being amazed, I was argumentative. Like Gideon, I had no idea how God could ever use me in the manner he was asking.

Keep in mind, this was many years ago when women's ministry programs were not the norm in churches. In fact, at my church, if you didn't sing in the choir or volunteer in the nursery, there really wasn't another place where women could serve or learn. The women in my church hungered for more of the Lord. I knew that. I was one of them. God called me to engage women so they could fall more in love with him. Inexperienced in church work, unprepared to serve women, and ill-equipped to lead, I called the church secretary and asked to meet with my pastor.

It might seem a little strange to think about God speaking to you. It was for Gideon. And it certainly was for me. I know God genuinely wants to reveal himself to his people—especially when we cry out to him. But how does he do that? It is different for everyone.

For some, he may speak in a small voice. For others, he may reveal himself through nature, people, or circumstances. Often he will speak directly through his word, the Bible. There are a million ways God can choose to reveal himself. One of the things that makes life so wild and wonderful is that God loves speaking to ordinary people like Gideon, me, and you.

Something occurred in Gideon that made the townspeople change their opinions of him. One minute they were calling him bad names and the next, they were following him into battle. What happened? Judges 6:34 says, "Then the Spirit of the Lord came upon Gideon…" These words represent a turning point in Gideon's life. The power of God transformed Gideon. Physically, he was still scrawny, but spiritually, he had become a mighty warrior, and the whole community saw the change.

Under-resourced and ill-prepared, the mighty warrior marched into battle. The Midianites' army consisted of 135,000 men while Gideon's army had only 300 men. The

Midianites possessed every kind of weapon. Gideon's army (instructed by God) used only trumpets and torches. The battle was short and decisive as God caused the enemy to turn on each other. The Bible says Gideon's army subdued the Midianites, and the land enjoyed peace. Gideon, the mighty warrior—along with his God—had surely prevailed.

TRANSFORMATION IS A PROCESS

I met with my pastor. He was thrilled at my willingness to implement a women's program. In fact, he was so excited he created a staff position for me at the church. I don't know if "women's ministry director" was God's new name for me, but I was called that in my new role. It is important to understand—God didn't just give me a new job, he was showing me a new path my life was about to take. He was showing me the clothes in my closet didn't matter.

I never dreamed more than twenty years later, I would still be serving God through ministry with women. Even more amazing is how God gave me a compassionate heart for women. I love working with women now. I'm a gal's gal.

Today, my identity isn't wrapped up in a women's ministry job. It's centered on the love of Jesus who loves women. I believe Jesus has asked me to love women like he loves them. And I'm trying. My hope is that each day I am getting better at loving people for Jesus' sake. Because when I do, transformation takes place.

The word "transformed" comes from the Greek word *metamorphoo*. You might recognize it from the root word metamorphosis. It means "to change after being with." An encounter with the Holy God will change you. This change may happen overnight or may be an on-going experience. Some encounters may be gigantic God moments. Other times, your encounter with God may be quiet and simple. In either case, this experience will be unique to you, and you will be different afterward. Gideon became a mighty warrior. I became a woman who loved serving and teaching women even more. Gideon's encounter with God was a life-changing event. Mine was a process.

Several years ago, I claimed 2 Corinthians 3:18 as my life verse. It is an amazing verse because it talks about becoming like Jesus through transformation. It says, "...we all reflect God's glory and are being transformed into his likeness..." This verse contains two important truths.

The first is that *our lives can be a reflection of God.* How? By living the way he wants us to live. I don't know about you, but I find this challenging because we are molded into the image of what we give priority. Our lives reflect the things we value. We look like what is most important in our lives. If our jobs, kids, technology, or one of a million other things are what we value most, then we reflect that. However, if we allow God to guide our lives, the things we do will bring him glory—and we will reflect him. This is a great privilege. The question we must ask ourselves is "What priority does my life reflect?"

The second truth from this great verse is that *our lives can be transformed to look like Jesus.* It means we will begin to take on the qualities and attributes Jesus exemplified. It is true we begin to look like those we hang around. For example, my friend Gina says a lot of cute words like "chitty-chat" (to talk). Not long after the first time I heard her say that phrase, I found myself repeating it to my family. Although Gina and I look nothing alike, I have found my mannerisms sometimes resemble hers. The more time we spend with Jesus, the more we will look like him.

I want to look like Jesus. And I want others to see that I look like him, too. When my son Jack was in college, he lived 14 hours from home. Most of his friends didn't know me. I had this hope that one day, he would have to describe me to his friends. I prayed the scenario would go something like this: *It's late at night. Jack and his roommate are visiting about life and "things." Somehow the conversation turns to family and more specifically, to mothers. The boys are joking about their mamas. Then the conversation turns a little more serious. Jack's roommate describes his mother and the way she cooks his favorite meal. Then it is Jack's turn to describe his favorite home-cooked meal, enchiladas. The roommate asks him, "What does your mom look like?" And Jack, as serious as he can be, says, "My mom? Oh, she looks a lot like Jesus."*

I don't think there is anything nerdy about looking like Jesus. In fact, if there was one photo in my graduation scrapbook I would relish, it would be the one where I looked just like Jesus.

GOD'S INVISIBLE QUALITIES

Gideon was neither mighty nor a warrior. Yet that's what God called him. God saw something in Gideon that no one else could see. But when the Spirit began to work in Gideon, he was changed. And others began to see a mighty warrior. God's invisible qualities were lived out in a man. His life began as a nerd but transformed into the qualities God saw in him. He was forever changed and because of that, the people around him were forever changed. His world became a better place.

As for me, I wasn't all that enamored with women, but God called me to love them anyway. God's invisible qualities were at work in a gal who cried out to him and who was willing to try and become more like him.

My hope and prayer continues to be that each day, I some-how, someway show Jesus to someone. I pray when others look at me, they see a Susan who loves Jesus so much that she is beginning to look like him.

The end of 2 Corinthians 3:18 says "(you) will be trans-formed into His likeness with ever-increasing glory." Ever-increasing glory is infinite. It means life with Jesus just keeps getting better. I believe, through my friendship with Jesus, he is making me better and better.

So if God had a scrapbook, there would be a photo of me in it. And Gideon. And you. And anyone else willing to be transformed into his likeness. God's scrapbook would be filled with photos of people who asked, "God, who do you want me to become?"

Holy transformation can happen to anyone. It occurs as a result of an encounter with God. Ask him to reveal himself to you. Allow him to let his invisible qualities become a real-ity in your life.

But be prepared to become shiny.

Living a transformed life will reflect God's glory, and oth-ers will see him lived out in you. That's transformation.

IMMEASURABLY MORE MEANS

* God uses ordinary people to accomplish his extraordinary purposes.
* God sees you, not as who you are, but what you can become.
* Others will see God living through you.

YOUR JESUS STORY

* Susan's life verse is 2 Corinthians 3:18. Would you be willing to research and discover a verse you think God might be claiming for you and your life?

* Use three words to describe yourself. Do you think God would use the same descriptive words for you?

* Do you sense God is leading you to step out of your comfort zone? What is stopping you?

Dear Lord,

Wow! I started off looking pretty rough. Thankfully, you have loved me through all my different looks! I'm talking about my spiritual looks as much as my physical looks. I was a sinner who needed a Savior. You came along, moved into my heart, and offered me a whole new look—inside and out. I am so thankful. My desire, Lord, is to look more like you each day. This is a difficult task, but with your help, I know I can do it. I pray that as I try to look more like you that others will see you living in me.

Amen.

chapter three

☀LOVE☀

A Different Kind of Love Story

*See what great love the Father has lavished on us,
that we should be called children of God!
And that is what we are!*

1 JOHN 3:1A

Immeasurably more means God lavishly loves you.

When my mom was six she was playing at a friend's house in her small hometown of Nash, Oklahoma. A thunderstorm was moving in so the friend's mother told Mom she needed to go home quickly before the storm came. Walking alone in Nash was not a safety issue in those days, so she put on her shoes and briskly walked down Main Street toward her home.

Halfway there, she realized she wasn't going to make it in time. The storm was moving in too quickly. Lightning cracked all around her. The rain poured down hard. Looking across the street, she saw a church on the corner so she ran to the front door. It was locked. Only the small stoop protected her from the now ravaging storm. Mom was more frightened than she had ever been. She began crying and wondered why she had ever left the safety of her friend's house.

After what seemed to be an eternity, Mom saw car lights coming towards the church. She recognized the car. It was her father's. In the pouring rain, he opened the door, got out and ran to her. He embraced her and carried her back to the safety of the car.

Mom told me this event, more than any other in her life, gave her a picture of her Heavenly Father's love. Her earthly father, out of love and concern, not only rescued her from the ravaging storm, but also carried her to safety. Through this, she saw a Heavenly Father who delighted in her and loved her, searched for her when she was lost, carried her during her storms, and ultimately delivered her.

Maybe your earthly father doesn't look so loving. It's possible he has failed you in some way or let you down. Perhaps you have never known an earthly father. Maybe an earthly father's love is unimaginable to you. Whatever circumstances surround you and your earthly father, please know you have a Heavenly Father who lavishes his love on you and calls you his child.

YOUR HEAVENLY FATHER LOVES YOU

When it comes to our Heavenly Father, he's all about love. In the Bible, after *Lord, God, Father,* and *Jesus Christ,* the word "love" is the second-most used word behind the word "heart." That's not really surprising since the Bible is all about God, and the Bible says God is love (1 John 4:8).

It would be interesting to know how often we use the word "love" in our everyday conversations. We certainly use it to share affection with people who are special to us.

But more times than not, we are careless with the word. We use it to describe how we feel about ordinary things like panda bears, pizza, and shoes.

God doesn't use the word so lightly. Love is the motivating force behind everything he does. We see this from the very first time love is mentioned in the Bible. There is a phrase Bible study scholars use called the *law of first mention*. This is when an important word is used for the first time in the Bible, and the subject remains unchanged in the mind of God and throughout scripture.

Along with a lot of other "firsts" (the first man, first woman, first sin, first rainbow), the word "love" is first mentioned in the book of Genesis. All these physical firsts set up the narrative of God and his great love story. He created man and woman because he loved being in relationship with people. When the first sin entered the world through Adam and Eve, God provided the first promise of redemption. He sent the first rainbow after the flood to promise that even though the world was broken, his love and mercy would always remain.

The Bible is a love story, although sometimes it doesn't feel like a love story because many of the stories appear to make God seem harsh and not very loving. That is why it's important when reading the Bible to always ask, *"What does God want me to know about him by reading this?"* This is especially true when looking at the first mention of the word "love."

TAKE YOUR SON, WHOM YOU LOVE

"Love" is first mentioned in Genesis 22:2: "Take your son, your only son, Isaac, whom you love…" These words seem oddly placed because immediately after God acknowledges Abraham's love for Isaac, he asks Abraham to sacrifice his son. Really? How can the first reference to love precede such a difficult task, especially when what God is asking sounds exactly like the opposite of love?

Hundreds—perhaps thousands—of Bible experts have written about the story of God, Abraham, and Isaac. I'm no theologian, but I *have* personally experienced God's love. Because of this, I think this story has a lot more to do with love than it does sacrifice.

> *God said to Abraham, "Take your only son, Isaac, whom you love. Sacrifice him as a burnt offering."*
> GENESIS 22:2, PARAPHRASED

This is a difficult verse to understand because in our culture, we know little about the sacrificial system of biblical times. In those days, the Law required parents to buy back their firstborn from God by offering a sacrificial lamb in his or her place. The lamb also needed to be the firstborn and without blemish, making it a valuable asset to the one who was sacrificing it.

In this particular account, God seems to be asking Abraham to sacrifice his son instead of a lamb. Would Abraham do it? It appears he would. But before we get to that part, let's go back to the law of first mention. The word "love" is used to set up the entire story (and I think the entire Bible). Here,

God's statement shows he understands Isaac is not only valuable to Abraham, but is also deeply loved by Abraham.

God acknowledges this love, which is probably one of the biggest ideas found in all of scripture. God knows what it is like to love an only son. Hear his words about Jesus: "This is my Son, whom I love; with him I am well pleased" (Matthew 3:17).

By acknowledging Abraham's love for Isaac, God is telling Abraham (and us) he values and deeply loves his children. What does God want you to know about him after reading about love and the law of first mention? Like Abraham, a father who loves his son, your Heavenly Father loves you because you are his child.

MY FATHER'S LOVE

I was a senior in high school. It was a Saturday night, and my boyfriend and I went to a party on a friend's farm. Shortly after we arrived, we got in a little fight. I was mad at him so I left the party and started walking down the dark farm road that led to the main street. It just so happened my friend Kevin was arriving at the party as I was walking down that dark road. He stopped and offered to take me home. I hopped in his car and off we went. We actually did not go straight home. We stopped at Denny's to have a snack. I'm not sure how long we were at the restaurant.

Meanwhile, my boyfriend was concerned. I had disappeared into thin air. He drove up and down the farm road with no luck finding me. Eventually he drove to my house to inform my father I was missing. The two of them went looking for me, but with no success. After searching the roads and asking other friends at the party, they returned to my house.

In the meantime, I didn't realize the angst people were having over my disappearance. After our late-night snack, Kevin drove me home. As we pulled into my long driveway, my father was standing there, waiting. Uh-oh. Even from a distance, I could see his face. I knew I was in big trouble.

Kevin pulled into the driveway and I got out of the car and quickly walked towards my dad. "I'm so sorry, Dad." The words were flowing out of my mouth.

As I approached my dad, he did something I never expected. He wrapped his arms around me and said, "I love you." That was it. The look of joy and relief on his face did not need any more words. He was looking at his little girl who was now safe. I was his child, the one he dearly loved.

Right then, my own father showed me what real love was like. It had nothing to do with what I said or did. My dad demonstrated he was a father who loved his child, no matter what the circumstances. That night, love had everything to do with my father. He didn't *choose* to love. He just loved me. After this experience, I came to understand why "love" is first mentioned in the story of Abraham and Isaac. God wants us to know he loves us just like a father loves his child.

STAY HERE... WE WILL COME BACK TO YOU

"Stay here… while I and the boy go over there. We will worship and then we will come back to you" (Genesis 22:5). Abraham tells his servants that *we* will come back to you. Let that sink in for a minute. Abraham did not say, "I will come back." It appears he had every intention of coming back with his son.

Abraham believed both he and Isaac would return even though there were so many things he did not know. He didn't know why God asked him to sacrifice. He didn't know what the outcome would be. He didn't know how God would provide. All Abraham knew was God loved him like a father loves a son. That was enough for Abraham to trust God. It was enough for him to tell his servants, "We will come back."

THE PHONE CALL

It was eleven o'clock in the evening. I had just gone to bed when my cell phone buzzed. It was my grown son texting me. "Do we have a family history of heart conditions?" I picked up the phone and called him. "Why? What's wrong with your heart?" I asked.

"Well, I'm experiencing some pain in my heart, and my arm is a little numb." I asked Jack what he had had for dinner (heart) and if he had been doing anything new in his activities (arm). Both responses provided potential reasons for his heart and arm ailment. However, the reality was it could be real heart issues.

I was in Kansas City and Jack was in Birmingham. It would be impossible for me to get to him before morning. Fortunately, Jack had a nurse friend living six blocks away. He promised to text and ask her to be on alert for the rest of the night. I suggested he prop himself up and try to rest. We hung up.

History was repeating itself. When Jack was in college, every now and then, he would text and ask me to solve some medical malady he was experiencing. Usually it was allergies. Now as I lay in bed, it was, yet again, one of those mother moments where I didn't have enough information and a whole night lay before me. Of course, I was hoping heartburn and the first day of softball practice were the culprits. But I couldn't be sure. I was about to face a very long night.

As I lay in bed, the story of Abraham and Isaac came to my mind. Like Abraham, I loved my only son. In the quiet of the moment, it was as if God was asking me, "Will you trust Jack with me? Will you give him to me?" In that moment, I had a decision to make. I could stay awake and worry about Jack all night. Or, I could give him over to my Heavenly Father (who I knew loved him) and let him watch over my son.

In more than 26 years as a mother, I had never felt so committed to my decision. In what I call my Abraham and Isaac moment, I handed my son over to God. I prayed: "Heavenly Father, I know you love Jack even more than I do. You are stronger, more powerful, and bigger than anything he will face tonight. So, tonight, Lord, he is yours. I'm giving him completely to you. I trust that whatever happens, it is because you are in charge, and you love your children." I rolled over and went to sleep.

The next morning I awoke at six. I texted Jack: "How are you feeling?"

"Great. After we talked, I went to sleep and didn't have any more trouble. My heart seems to be feeling just fine," he said.

I'm convinced this incident had nothing to do with Jack. I believe this experience was meant for me to learn something about God. Out of concern for my son, God was reminding me how much he loved me. Just like he said to Abraham, God also said to me, "Susan, take your son, your only son, Jack, whom you love, and offer him to me." In that quiet time, I knew God was reminding me how my mother's love was similar to his love for me.

And not only did God love me, he loved my son, too. Because of that, I knew I could trust him with my precious son. What I learned about God that night was his love gives me the power to trust him with things I value.

ABRAHAM LOOKED AND, IN A THICKET, HE SAW A RAM

It appears Abraham was willing to sacrifice his son. But as the story unfolds, God steps in and provides a substitute sacrifice for Isaac. "Abraham looked up and there in a thicket he saw a ram caught by its horns" (Genesis 22:13). God had provided a ram for Abraham. This one act of God providing a substitute in the story of Abraham and Isaac sets up the outline for the world's greatest love story.

God wasn't asking Abraham to give up his son. Instead, God was taking Abraham to a place of trust—of belief. Without belief, it is difficult to experience our Heavenly Father's rich love.

People often ask why they should read and study the Old Testament. There are many reasons to read the Old Testament but when you read it along with the New Testament, it allows you to see God's love story in its entirety. This is especially true in the story of Abraham and Isaac.

When it looked like there was no other solution but to offer Isaac as a sacrifice, God provided Abraham with a ram. On a much bigger scale, when the world had no way to escape eternal death and separation from our Heavenly Father, he stepped in. God gave us his son. The perfect and unblemished lamb named Jesus would be the sacrifice for all of God's children.

> *This is how God showed his love among us:*
> *He sent his one and only Son into the world*
> *that we might live through him.*
> 1 JOHN 4:9

> *For God so loved the world that he gave*
> *his one and only Son, that whoever believes in him*
> *shall not perish but have eternal life.*
> JOHN 3:16

God loves you so much he sacrificed his only son, Jesus, for you. He was willing to do for you what Abraham did not have to do for Isaac. When you read the beautiful story of Abraham and Isaac, you are really reading about the love of Jesus.

How much does God love you? So much he would give his most valuable possession for you. He would move heaven and earth for you. He delights in you. You are the apple of his eye. You are the one he claims as his child. You are cherished. Your God is a Heavenly Father who loves you lavishly and extravagantly.

GOD STOPPED A SNOWSTORM

The writer, David, talks about how much God lavishly and extravagantly loved him in Psalm 18. Under attack and in distress, David called out to the Lord. The Lord heard him, and here's what God did:

* He shook the foundations of the mountains.
* He parted the heavens and came down.
* He shot his arrows and scattered the enemies.
* He reached down and drew David from the deep waters and rescued him from his powerful enemies.

In verse 19, David explains why God rescued him. Please don't miss this.

He brought me out into a spacious place;
he rescued me because he delighted in me.
PSALM 18:19

God was willing to move heaven and earth, eliminate the enemy and rescue his beloved because *he delighted in him.* He will do the same for you and me. I know because one time, I experienced a similar rescue.

While my mother was wintering in Florida, she fell and broke her hip. It was late January, and I flew down to bring her home to Kansas City, where we both lived. A few days after I arrived, it was time to return home with Mom and her newly repaired hip. The weather forecast was not good. It was raining in Florida and a major snowstorm was about to blast the Midwest. The meteorologists were predicting between six and twelve inches of snow—a significant snowstorm.

Mom was frail. She had many health issues but the biggest challenge facing her at the present time was an airplane ride with a very tender hip. I was anxious about the weather and the possible delays it might cause. A layover in Memphis added to the stress because sleet and ice were expected there. Missing our connection in Memphis meant we would most likely spend the night in a hotel.

The additional travel and movement would certainly be extremely painful for Mom and could potentially add to her other health issues. My anxiety escalated as I spoke with friends in Kansas City who advised me to reconsider bringing her home.

On the morning of our flight, I spent some time alone with God. During this time, God reminded me of some things I had been learning about him back in Kansas City. A group of women and I had been studying the Old Testament book of Daniel. One of the main themes of Daniel is God is sovereign over everything, and he is able to do great things because he is great. My reading in Psalm 18 that morning reminded me not only was God *able* to do great things, He is also *willing* to do great things.

As I was pondering these big thoughts, I realized God is no less powerful today than he was during the Old Testament times. Believing God is powerful and fully capable of miracles, I asked my great God to please stop the snow from falling in Kansas City so my mother and I could return quickly and safely home. With that prayer request tucked in my mind and heart, we departed for the airport. It was pouring rain.

We boarded the plane and readied ourselves for the first part of our trip to Memphis. Waiting for takeoff, I called my girlfriend in Kansas City for a weather update. She told me the snow was coming, but nothing was happening yet. Upon departure, the pilot shared his pleasantries, followed by a brief weather forecast for Memphis: sleet and ice. We traveled the 90-minute flight with little turbulence and no trouble and landed safely in a chilly, damp—but not icy—Memphis.

With no delay, we changed planes. As soon as we were settled in our seats for the next flight, I made a quick phone call to my girlfriend for one last weather update. She said, "Susan, it's odd. The weather forecasters have predicted the snow should be here by now, but nothing is happening. It's just overcast and cold."

By the time we arrived in Kansas City, our spirits were up. Though temperatures were frigid, only light snow flurries were in the air. There was no measurable snowfall. We had made it safely!

The following day, while reading the newspaper, I came across a little article hidden on page eight. I almost didn't notice the sidebar story, but the headline caught my attention. It said: "Heavy snows misses Kansas City area." The reporter wrote: "A potent winter storm dumped up to ten inches of snow in southeast Kansas, closing schools and causing hazardous driving conditions."

The piece went on to tell how the storm pushed through central Missouri, creating near whiteout conditions in a small town outside of the Kansas City metro area. The story continued by saying that although eight to ten inches of snow were reported in most areas surrounding Kansas City, the metro did not receive the significant snowfall that had been predicted.

After reading the article, I got out a map and charted all the places and towns mentioned in this story. Looking on the map at the path of the snowfall, I was amazed. Significant snowfall had occurred completely around the city. Yet, Kansas City received no snow. God had stopped a snowstorm. I believe he did it for me.

It was as simple as this: Ten inches of snow was predicted in Kansas City, but it didn't happen. On that day, God decided to extend grace to his anxious, yet believing, child. He said, "Yes, Susan, I can stop a snowstorm in Kansas City. And today, I am going to do that for you because I delight in you. I love you, child."

Since then, God has not done anything for me quite as miraculous as stopping a snowstorm. I can't explain why he chose to stop this snowstorm knowing it disrupted nature and potentially had a negative effect on others like hardware stores and snow removal companies.

But here's what I do know. God loves me. And he loves everyone else too. He doesn't love me more than the hardware store owner or the snow removal man. But, on that particular day, it was God's will to grant my request. On another day, he was willing to move heaven and earth for David. He will do nothing less for you.

God is in the business of love. If one were to summarize the Bible in seven words, I think they would be:

God loves you
Love God
Love others

It's really as simple as that.

FINAL THOUGHTS

Looking over this chapter, I realize it begins and ends with stories about storms. It makes me wonder if perhaps God reveals his love for us especially during the storms in our lives. Are you are experiencing a storm in your life right now? If so, remember the most basic fact about God: He is love.

The first mention of love in scripture speaks of a father who loves. This is your Father. He loves you. He provides for you. He will move heaven and earth for you. You are his child.

IMMEASURABLY MORE MEANS

* God's love came first. He loved you even before you knew him.

* There is nothing you can do to make God love you. He just does, no matter the circumstances.

* God loves to love you because he delights in you.

* God is the giver of love and of life. Through the love of his son, God gave you life.

YOUR JESUS STORY

* Write about a time when you knew God loved you. Share your story with someone.

* You have heard the verse so often it seems to get watered down. When you realize John 3:16 is the New Testament story describing exactly what happens in the story of Abraham and Isaac, what does John 3:16 really mean to you?

* When you believe in God, the Bible says you are his child. How does this truth enable you to live your life differently?

Dear loving Father,

You call me your child. You love me lavishly—so much so that I am called a child of the King. You delight in me. You bless me. You favor me. You highly esteem me. I believe you, God, when you say your love is higher, deeper, wider, and longer than eternity because your love has no end. I know there is no way you can love me any more because your love for me is complete. Words cannot express how grateful I am for the perfect example of love you set before me. So, Lord, teach me to love that way—the way you love. I want to love you—and others—the way you love me. In your steadfast love I pray,

Amen.

 LIFE

Handwritten Letters

For the word of God is alive and active.
HEBREWS 4:12

Immeasurably more means God's words speak life into you because they are alive and active.

I was in college, about to get married, when I received a letter from my dad. It was the only letter he had ever written me.

When I picked it up from the mailbox, I immediately knew who it was from. In the letter, my dad gave me fatherly advice about becoming a bride. He reminded me that he valued me as his daughter and enjoyed spending time with me. He closed the letter by telling me how much he loved me.

More than thirty years later, that letter is one of my most prized possessions. I have read it countless times. I still value the advice in it. And I cherish the hand who wrote it. My dad is no longer with me. But his written words give me a lasting reminder that I am his daughter, and he loves me.

The Bible is like God's handwritten letter to us. In it, God tells us he loves us. He promises to be our Heavenly Father who never gives up on us. He reminds us we are created in his image so we can learn to mirror his wonderful attributes.

He says he dreams bigger dreams for us than we can imagine. In God's letter, he comforts us and keeps a record of all our tears. He values us. He equips us. He sent his son for us. The Bible is like a sourcebook for everything we will face. It's unique because it is written for *anyone* who reads it.

One of the reasons I began reading the Bible as part of my regular routine was the example set by my Auntie Ann. I saw firsthand how consistently she read the Bible, and I saw the value she placed on the words in it.

AUNTIE ANN'S REGULAR HABIT

My sister Mary noticed the light was still on in Auntie Ann's room. Thinking my aunt had fallen asleep, Mary quietly entered her room to turn it off. However, instead of sleeping, my aunt was doing something she had done every day for more than 50 years. She was reading her Bible.

Just a few hours before, Auntie Ann had called my sister on the telephone. "Mary, I can't remember things and I'm scared." My sister assured her things would be okay.

Shortly after, Mary arrived at her house. She found Auntie Ann frustrated, scared, and tired. Mary helped her pack a bag. They closed up the house and returned to my sister's home. By the time they arrived at Mary's house, it was late evening. Mary helped Auntie Ann get settled in the guest room and left her there to get ready for bed.

Mary shared with me later, "Susan, it was amazing. Even though Ann's mind has faded, her love and passion for God's word has not."

Hearing the story reminded me of all the times I had personally seen Auntie Ann read the Bible. For my aunt, these were not merely words on paper; they were life. These words got her through each day. When my aunt struggled, she sought comfort in the powerful words. When she felt alone, she found a friend in the pages. I know this is true because my aunt spoke often about the power of God's written words in her life.

I want to be like my aunt. Later in my life, if I become confused and can't remember things, I pray God's words will be the *one* thing that comes naturally and automatically to my mind.

THE KING WHO ACCIDENTALLY DISCOVERED THE BIBLE

There was a man in the Bible named Josiah. Unlike my dear Auntie Ann, reading the Bible did not come naturally to him because he didn't even know the Bible existed.

Josiah became king when he was eight years old. The Bible says, "He did what was right in the eyes of the Lord…" (2 Chronicles 34:2). This is an interesting fact because the Bible says both Josiah's father and grandfather did evil in the eyes of the Lord. Josiah's early influencers did detestable things and worshiped idols. Yet, Josiah began to seek God when he was just sixteen years old.

Even though his father and grandfather were not role models of faith, Josiah still served his God. We cannot be sure how Josiah's faith was nurtured. But the Bible gives us a clue. The story of Josiah is told in 2 Kings and 2 Chronicles. The accounts are almost identical, with the exception of one small detail. In 2 Kings 22:1, we are told that Josiah's mother's name was Jedidah.

In this case, Jedidah's name appears immediately before we are told that Josiah "did what was right in the eyes of the Lord" (2 Kings 22:2). There appears to be a direct link between these two facts—Jedidah his mother and doing right in the eyes of the Lord.

It is just possible Josiah was influenced by this woman mentioned only one time in scripture. This is such an encouragement, especially if you are a mother, aunt, or grandmother. Your influence speaks volumes in the lives of young people, even when bad influences surround them.

When Josiah was twenty-six years old, he began to clean out the temple, which had fallen into disarray. In biblical times, the temple was considered the dwelling place of God. It was Israel's most holy place. The Israelites had fallen far away from God, and the temple was practically in ruins. Josiah enlisted men to repair and clean the temple. While the workers were cleaning, they found "the Book of the Law." This book consisted of the first five books of the Bible, and was Israel's Bible, which had been lost for many years.

The workers took the Bible to Josiah. One of them began to read the words written in the book. When Josiah heard the words, he was grieved because he knew he and his people had not kept the laws of the book "Great is the LORD's anger that is poured out on us because our fathers have not kept the word of the LORD; they have not acted in accordance with all that is written in this book" (2 Chronicles 34:21b).

We don't know which words were read to Josiah. But upon hearing them, Josiah realized how little his people knew about God. This made him very sad. After hearing God's words that day, Josiah "read all the words of the Book of the Covenant" (2 Kings 23:2). Then he committed "...to follow the LORD and to keep his commands, regulations, and decrees with all his heart and all his soul..." (2 Kings 23:3). He did this for the rest of his life.

King Josiah didn't even know about God's words until he was twenty-six years old. But as soon as he heard the words, he knew they were the words of God.

I'm grateful to Josiah because he taught me I am never too old or too unknowledgeable to begin reading the Bible.

Josiah began reading the Bible and continued reading it for as long as he lived. Auntie Ann read the Bible as part of her daily routine even when she couldn't remember other things.

These two examples have inspired me to make Bible reading a regular lifetime habit. I discovered the Bible is not some old book that looks great on a coffee table. I have grown to love this ancient book because it's timeless and relevant for today.

The Bible's truths are packed with wisdom for my everyday life. It teaches me about God so I can know him better. In it, his words are alive and powerful. I pray you will allow him to show you his immeasurably more through his written words.

GOD'S WORDS ARE ALIVE AND POWERFUL

For the word of God is alive and powerful...
HEBREWS 4:12a NLT

Not long ago, I visited my friend Amy, who lives in another state. Amy's home overlooks the most beautiful lake with mountains surrounding it. The view is breathtaking.

One evening as the sun slowly set, we sat on her porch, anticipating nature's show. I had been visiting her for almost a week and up to this point, we had been talking nearly nonstop.

As we settled in on her porch, I noticed a lack of peace on my friend's face. The spectacular oranges, reds, and yellows of the sunset were taking second place to Amy's thoughts.

"What are you thinking about?" I asked.

"Elizabeth. She has a doctor's appointment tomorrow to see if the clots are gone." Months before, Amy's daughter Elizabeth had been diagnosed with blood clots in both of her legs and her lungs. The healing had come much slower than anticipated.

Amy had just spoken on the phone with Elizabeth. She had had a CT scan performed earlier in the day, and the lab had sent the disc of images home with her so she could take them to her doctor the next day. Elizabeth is a take-charge young lady, so when she returned home, she immediately put the disc in her computer and looked at the results. On the phone, she told her mom she was not surprised to see black spots all over her lungs because her chest hurt, and she just knew the clots were not going away.

Amy and I faced twilight wondering about the outcome of the next day when Elizabeth would again see the doctor. After some time of silence, we agreed praying might relieve some nervous energy.

We remembered Jesus has instructed us to ask. We knew *asking* God to answer our prayer is so much more powerful than just *wishing* for things to happen. As twilight approached, Amy and I decided to ask God to heal Elizabeth of the blood clots in her lungs instead of just wishing everything was going to be okay.

Recalling that Scripture says, "God's words are alive and powerful" (Hebrews 4:12), we decided to pray using *his* words instead of our own. We chose the psalmist's prayer called out by David in Psalm 91. This Psalm is a battle cry. It speaks of God's protection.

Amy and I resolved to be armed like warriors as we prayed. "Heavenly Father, you are our refuge, our fortress, and our God, in whom we trust." Our words became stronger and bolder as we prayed. "Deliver Elizabeth from the snare of the fowler and from the deadly pestilence of the blood clots in her lungs." Our voices raised. "We will not fear the terror of the night nor the arrow that flies by day."

We claimed God's promises as we cried out: "I (God) will deliver Elizabeth. I will protect Elizabeth because she knows my name." And we trusted in God's faithfulness. "I (God) will be with Elizabeth in trouble and will rescue her and honor her." Amen.

As we said God's words aloud, we knew we were saying more than just words. We were claiming promises from our

God's words. We trusted his words. And as the darkness of evening came, our resolve became firm. In those quiet moments of sunset, we called out to God and could feel his presence.

The next morning Elizabeth called. "No clots in the lungs! The doctor said the black spots were normal markings on the lungs."

We will never know if praying God's words removed Elizabeth's clots. It doesn't matter. Just the night before, two battle-crying women trusted God's words. Our prayers were answered long before the doctor's appointment the next morning. God answered our prayers the moment we prayed. He reminded us he would protect, rescue, and honor Elizabeth. Praying God's words had poured an unexplainable peace over us, reminding us his words truly are alive and powerful.

One of the ways I have found that God makes scripture come alive is by reading it out loud. The Psalms offer great words of encouragement and praise. Try reading a Psalm and place your name in the reading. The scriptures not only come alive, but become personal to you. It is as if God is saying these words to you.

There is a sample of this at the end of this chapter for you to try. When you do this, God is literally speaking life into your words.

GOD WILL GIVE HIS WORDS TO YOU

I have put my words in your mouth.
JEREMIAH 1:9b

The worst thing that can happen to a public speaker happened to me. I was scheduled to speak during one of the breakout sessions at a women's conference. My session was assigned for Saturday morning.

On Friday night, I attended the conference as a participant excited to hear the keynote speaker. As she approached the stage, she asked us to open our Bibles to Ruth 1:1. Hmmm. Ruth was the Scripture I was planning to use the next day. I thought, "Well, this will be a nice tie-in to my topic."

The keynote speaker continued with her talk. It was uncanny. Point by point and verse by verse, she covered the topic almost precisely how I was planning to share it in my session the next day. My heart began to pound. Women would come to my session and hear almost the same message.

I excused myself from the table, ran to my car, sped home, and collapsed on the sofa where my husband was leisurely watching television. "You are never going to believe this!" I spewed. "The speaker tonight used the exact passage and said the same things I was going to share tomorrow. And to top it off, she said it all better than I would have!" I continued to lament. "Now, what am I going to do?"

My husband, who was still a little shell-shocked from my early arrival home and my panicked tone, calmly put the television on mute. "Susan, obviously God has a special message someone needs to hear. You must go up to your office, and ask him to give you special words." Then, sweetly, my husband placed his hands on my head and asked God to give me these special words.

Needless to say, I was still a little anxious the next day. I was not overly prepared. But even more, I felt like I was on a special mission from God (that's enough to make a person nervous). According to my husband, there was someone in the audience who needed to hear a message from God, and I was the vessel to present the words! I felt so small.

A sweet young high school girl named Elizabeth (yes, the same Elizabeth from earlier in the chapter) was my designated helper. She prayed these God words over me: "In their hearts humans plan their course, but the LORD establishes their steps" (Proverbs 16:9).

She had no idea how prophetic her prayer was about to become.

The time had come. Last night's fright and today's anxiety were behind me. The Holy Spirit had taken over. For almost an hour, I shared my new talk. At the completion of the session, a woman I barely knew approached me. "I don't know if anyone else was in the room because it was as if you were speaking only to me. Today, you said exactly what I needed to hear from God." As I stood with this woman, I silently praised God for giving me his words.

It is true that God's words can become your words. When faced with a situation where you don't know what to say, knowing God's words can give you the words, no matter the situation or circumstance.

As a speaker, my worst day turned into one of my best. God had shown me how his words can do immeasurably more than I could have ever done. God had put his words in my mouth.

God will put his words in your mouth, too. The more time you spend reading his words, the more you are apt to repeat them. If you are in a situation where you feel you do not have the right words to say, seek them out in scripture. Look up key words such as faith, courage, or hope in the back of your Bible. There are a variety of scriptures that speak to the very issue you are seeking. Once you have found a verse, allow God to speak that verse through you. Then his words become yours!

READING THE BIBLE

When I read a book, I have what I call the 300-page rule. If a book has more than 300 pages, I'm not very interested in reading it. My Bible has 1,950 pages! That's more than six times the number of pages in my reading rule. However, the Bible is a compilation of sixty-six books. When I think about it this way, reading the Bible is possible. For example, Genesis only has 83 pages. Totally doable.

Reading the Bible may seem hard. I get that. At first, the Bible seemed like (to me) a big book of rules and one-liner promises. It felt like a book of dos and don'ts. But when I really began to read it, I learned about a God who loves and values me. This made me want to read it more.

Several years ago, I wanted to read the Bible all the way through. To help me, I found a book with a reading plan that guided me through the Bible in a year. On January 1, I began on page one: Genesis chapter one.

I read earnestly for the first few weeks. Then I got distracted somewhere in Leviticus where it talks about infectious skin diseases and mildew and was defeated from reaching my goal. I tried several more times. I knew I needed help if I was going to accomplish my goal.

That's when I asked God to help me read his words. My desire was there, but my discipline was lacking. I asked God to wake me up each day so I could turn to his words first thing. I'm not exactly sure how this happened, but I am convinced that God's Spirit helped me stay committed until I finally made it all the way through the Bible. It took three years to read the entire Bible. But I read every page of God's words. And then I started over.

Don't worry about your ability to finish the Bible in a year or even your wisdom to understand everything written in it. Just open the book and start reading. When Auntie Ann did this, it became a lifetime habit. When Josiah read the Bible, he became devoted.

When I finished reading the entire Bible the first time, I discovered it wasn't an outdated book about people from days gone by. I fell in love with many of the people who shared their journeys.

Some of them are included in this book—the woman at the well, Gideon, Abraham, Josiah, to name a few. I realized these people lived real lives and had real stories to tell. I discovered most of these folks were ordinary people who longed to know their God better.

Those I read about had become a part of God's bigger story. After reading the Bible all the way through, I wondered: if God were to update the Bible—add 21st century people to it, would I be in it? Would my ordinary and simple story be part of God's story? It's totally possible.

I've learned from reading the Bible that God wants everyone to be a part of his story.

Years have passed since my first complete Bible reading. To date, I have read the Bible many more times. Somewhere along the line it moved from being a duty to becoming a privilege. Most days, I open it in anticipation to see what God might want to say to me that day or who he might want me to meet. This is what makes the Bible so fascinating. You never know who's going to show up in scripture. We learn about so many—the good, the bad, and the ugly.

The Bible says it "is useful to teach us what is true and to make us realize what is wrong in our lives. It corrects us when we are wrong and teaches us to do what is right" (2 Timothy 3:16, NLT). The Bible is an instruction manual about how to live life well. It guides us and keeps us on the right path. It teaches us to make better choices. It encourages us to love well and know that we are loved too.

But even more than teaching us, the Bible points us always to the most breathtaking attribute of God—that he loves us. He gave the biggest sacrifice, his son Jesus, so we could be part of his story. So every time I pick up the Bible and read, I can't help but think of how my life is so immeasurably more because I am a part of God's bigger story. So are you.

Want to know God better? Read the Bible. Want to learn about his will for your life? Read the Bible. Want to hear about God's great love for you? Read the Bible.

God's words are life.

They are powerful.

They are instructional.

They are alive.

They are proven.

They are comforting.

They are promises.

They are God's confirmation that he wants to connect with us.

IMMEASURABLY MORE MEANS

* The Bible is God's word written to you so that you may know him better.

* You don't have to understand everything written in the Bible; you just need to be obedient to reading it and willing to learn about it.

* God's words are as alive and relevant today as they were thousands of years ago when they were written. They equip you and help you try to do life like Jesus.

YOUR JESUS STORY

* What is keeping you from reading the Bible? Would you be willing to just start?

* Try praying/saying God's words. Look up Psalm 37:1-9. Insert your name by personalizing the verses. (See example below)

* 2 Timothy 3:16-17 says *"All Scripture is God-breathed and is useful for teaching, rebuking, correcting and training in righteousness so that the person of God may be thoroughly equipped for every good work."* Do you believe that God's words equip you for every good work as promised in this verse? When was there a time the Bible was helpful to you in your circumstances? What is something you are facing today?

* How might the Bible be able to equip you?

* Start reading the Bible using one of these reading plans:

  ⇒ Read the Book of John—one chapter a day will take you three weeks to complete.

  ⇒ Read Proverbs for a month (the book of wisdom). There are thirty-one chapters.

  ⇒ Read the New Testament in a year. Read one chapter a day/five days a week and you will complete the entire New Testament in a year.

  ⇒ Read the entire Bible in a year. Purchase *The One Year Bible* to use as a reading guide.

MAKE SCRIPTURE PERSONAL TO YOU

Read the following passage aloud using your name.

Psalm 37:1-9

(Insert your name), do not fret because of those who are evil or be envious of those who do wrong; for like the grass they will soon wither, like green plants they will soon die away.

(Insert your name), trust in the Lord and do good; dwell in the land and enjoy safe pasture.

(Insert your name), take delight in the Lord, and he will give you **(me)** the desires of your **(my)** heart.

(**Insert your name**), commit your way to the Lord; trust in him and he will do this: He will make your (**my**) righteous reward shine like the dawn, your (**my**) vindication like the noonday sun.

(**Insert your name**), be still before the Lord and wait patiently for him;

(**Insert your name**), do not fret when people succeed in their ways, when they carry out their wicked schemes.

(**Insert your name**), refrain from anger and turn from wrath; do not fret—it leads only to evil. For those who are evil will be destroyed, but those who hope in the Lord will inherit the land.

Dear Living Word,

You created everything through your spoken word. You gave me written words so I would know how to become more like you and be more prepared for this life. You became the Living Word so I could know you better. Because your words are alive and powerful, they speak life into my life. Help me, God, to pursue you through both your written word, by reading your Scriptures; and the Living Word, by following Jesus' examples. Thank You, God, for always pursuing me in ways that help me know you better.

Amen.

chapter five

✽ CHILDLIKE FAITH ✽

Lessons from a Two-year-old

...unless you return to square one and start over like children, you're not even going to get a look at the kingdom, let alone get in. Whoever becomes simple and elemental again, like this child, will rank high in God's kingdom.
MATTHEW 18:3-4 (THE MESSAGE)

Immeasurably more means Jesus treasures your childlike faith because it expands your vision of him.

A few years ago, I was asked in a group setting, "Who is the most influential person in your life?" Without pause, I replied, "My son, Jack." Over the years, I have learned many lessons about faith from my son. In a variety of ways, he is so much wiser than me. Watching him grow up showed me how a young person's faith can be so simple and pure. It reminded me that this is the kind of faith God desires.

The Lord blessed my husband and me with only one child. He was an easy child. I think it was because God knew one really-easy-child was all I could handle. I was a novice mom who had never really been around babies. They were a curiosity to me. In the hospital, when given the choice of staying an extra day or going home, I chose the extra day. I was scared to take my new baby home. When the time came for us to leave the hospital, my husband and I flipped a coin to decide who would dress the new baby. (I lost.) I'm convinced when Jack was born, the Lord just shook his head at me and then crossed his fingers.

Jack's birth changed me. Having a child adjusted the way I viewed life. It was as if a switch on my eyelids turned on. As a new mother, I was able to see life through my own eyes, as well as gain new perspectives by seeing things like a child again.

I remember our first trip to Toys "R" Us after Jack was born. My husband and I were shopping for his first Christmas present. We hadn't visited a toy store since we were young. Steve and I were like kids—ooohing and aaaahing at all the cool toys that had been invented since we were little. We looked like idiots because we stopped anyone who would join in our excitement over the newest and greatest.

After walking every aisle, touching every toy, and experiencing each and every gadget, we finally decided on the perfect gift for our one-year-old son: Lincoln Logs. Mind you, it would be another four years until the child could play with them, but they brought back a ton of happy memories for both of us. That trip to the Toys "R" Us store took us back to our childhood. Now with a child of my own, the toy store trip was only the beginning of the many experiences where I would have the opportunity to be childlike again.

THE GROCERY STORE AND THE SHOES

Jack was almost three when we lived in the Kansas City area. I was taking a break from full-time employment to stay home and learn lessons from my son. On this particular day, we had been playing at the house all morning. Now it was afternoon. We needed to go to the grocery store so we would have something to make for supper that evening. I placed Jack's red Converse® tennis shoes in front of him and asked him to put them on. Then I went to the kitchen to make our grocery list.

When I returned from the kitchen, I discovered that in all the time I had been gone, Jack had only managed to get one shoe on. Apparently, the piddling from the morning had continued on into the afternoon. I was a little agitated because I was ready to go. "Jack, why don't you have both shoes on? Why are you taking so long?" He looked at me and innocently asked, "Mom, why are we in a hurry to get to the grocery store?"

Gulp. We weren't in a hurry. In fact, the grocery store was the only big agenda item on our schedule for the day. What was my rush? Hadn't I chosen time off to spend with my son? Why couldn't I just slow down and enjoy?

Smiling at him, I sat down on the floor and savored the moment. Those cute tennis shoes and his sweet face were priceless. As we sat on the floor, we sang a song (that we made up) about putting on red Converse® tennis shoes.

My girlfriend Peggy once cross-stitched a sampler for me that says, "Hurry slowly." I love this phrase. It reminds me that even when life is busy, or we just need to get everyday stuff done, we can still slow down and savor the moments. The idea of hurry slowly teaches us even though we react with urgency to the things in our lives, we can still take a deliberate and thoughtful approach.

It has been more than twenty-five years since my son and I sat on the floor singing about red tennis shoes. I'm sure we made it to the grocery store just fine that day. I really can't remember. But I do remember a little boy, his shoes, and a song we made up together.

CHILDLIKE FAITH REMINDS US TO HURRY SLOWLY

There are approximately 400 years separating the Old Testament from the New Testament. Many scholars call this time the "silent years" because it's the time between the last inspired writings of the prophets and the beginning writings of the New Testament writers. During those years, God seemed to be very silent. In the book of Galatians, Paul says, "But when the time had fully come, God sent his Son…" (Galatians 4:4).

For 400 years, God had chosen to be silent. Now he was ready to speak. He did this through the birth of his Son.

A young, newlywed couple named Joseph and Mary returned to their hometown to register for the census. Mary, who was nine months pregnant, traveled with Joseph to Bethlehem in order to fulfill their obligation. By the time they arrived in the city, there were no motel rooms available. Inconvenient as it seems, it was time for the baby to be born.

Upon his arrival, Mary wrapped her new baby son in cloths and placed him in a manger. Angels appeared in the heavens and told shepherds who were working in the fields "a Savior has been born to you; he is Christ the Lord" (Luke 2:11). The Bible says "the shepherds *hurried* off and found Mary and Joseph" (Luke 2:16).

Imagine how Mary must have felt during this time. Surely she was overjoyed. Like any mother, Mary now had the chance to care for and love the cutest baby she had ever seen! But I wonder if Mary was also overwhelmed by the sacredness of the moment—knowing she had given birth to the Savior? Did she wonder how they were going to raise God? Was she curious about the strangers (shepherds) who came to pay a call on her baby? Did she ask God, "How in the world will I ever manage all this?"

We don't know if or how God answered Mary's questions. However, the Gospel of Luke records how Mary responded: "But Mary treasured up all these things and pondered them in her heart" (Luke 2:19). Pondered. *Webster's Dictionary* defines ponder as "to consider especially quietly, soberly, and deeply." Certainly Mary had every reason to be in a hurry and anxious. In the midst of the seriousness, the busyness, and the uncertainty of the situation, she quietly, soberly, and deeply enjoyed the preciousness of the moment.

There was much to be done in the coming days. But it could wait. Mary didn't want to miss the moment. So Mary slowed. She savored. She sang. In the stillness of a stable, Mary took a few minutes and just enjoyed her child.

I love the contrast of the responses of the shepherds and Mary in Jesus' birth story. The shepherds *hurried* while Mary *pondered*. Both responses were correct. Each of us must decide what is worth the hurry and what is worth the wait.

Mary shows us to take time to savor. I often want to rush through things and hurry my schedule. Yet, if I do this, I might miss something of value. Jesus wants us to experience the fullness of life, but when we hurry from one activity to another, it's easy to miss the moment.

Mary had every reason to move on and do things quickly. She was now raising the Savior of the world. Of all people, she had every reason to hurry. However, through her example, Mary reminds us sometimes we just need to ponder.

There are certainly times when hurrying is appropriate. The shepherds demonstrate this. Once they received the good news, they hurried to Jesus. What a great lesson for us today.

* What if when problems arise in our lives, we rush to Jesus, who has experienced everything we will ever face?

* What if when we are lonely, we hurry to Jesus because he is our friend and companion?

* What if when we feel undervalued and unloved, we run to the One who loves us unconditionally and eternally?

We often hurry to the things that are placed right before our eyes, taking little notice if it is even worth rushing towards. The shepherds remind us what is worth the hurry. They left their flocks so they could see their savior.

A life with Jesus helps us notice the simple, yet important, things. Maybe God has a special moment planned just for you at the grocery store this afternoon. Will you stop and notice?

CHILDLIKE FAITH TEACHES US TO FACE OUR FEARS

It was February of Jack's senior year. He had narrowed his college selection down to two schools. One was near, familiar, and comfortable. The other was far, unfamiliar, and unknown. For Jack, the far-away one seemed scary and risky.

One day he came downstairs from his room and joined me in the kitchen He had an announcement: "I have decided which college is right for me." He chose far away. All along I knew Jack preferred the school far away so I asked him how he made the decision.

"Even though going to a school far away makes me a little afraid, I realize I need to face that fear head on. It's the school I think is right for me, and I am willing to be a little scared in order to do the right thing." Jack hadn't come to this decision haphazardly. He had claimed Proverbs 16:9 as his verse for his senior year: "In his heart, man plans his course, but the Lord establishes his steps." He prayed about his decision. And he had faith, knowing God planned good things for his life.

Our entire family sought God about Jack's future. We asked God to show us signs of confirmation after the decision was made. When he began to tell people he was attending Auburn University, we were amazed at how many of our friends had connections there. It seemed like everyone we told had some good story about Auburn.

When one of Jack's closest friends also decided to attend the same school, we knew he would have someone from home nearby. We believed all these little things were God's way of confirming Jack's college decision. During this time, we kept our eyes on Jesus allowing him to navigate Jack's path. After his decision was made, he never looked back.

YOU MAY JUST WALK ON WATER

I have heard of only two people who have walked on water. One was Jesus. The other was his disciple Peter. Picture the scene with me. It was a stormy night. Darkness surrounded them, winds howled wildly around them, and fear consumed them. Still, Peter got out of the boat. He walked on water—to Jesus. The Bible doesn't say it, but I think Peter got out of that boat because he knew the power of Jesus was greater than the fear he possessed.

What do you think Peter will remember the next day, month, and year after he walked on the water? I think he will remember the adrenaline rush he experienced right before he climbed out of the boat. He will remember the smile on his face from knowing he actually walked on water. What a thrill to do something so scary, especially when it involves Jesus!

Before Peter walked on water, Jesus challenged the disciples: "Take courage! It is I. Don't be afraid" (Matthew 14:27). In essence, Jesus is saying, "Look to me instead of looking at your fears."

Several years ago when I was considering starting a ministry for women, I was afraid of failure. A dear friend reminded me true failure would be *not* pursuing what God had in mind for me. Facing my fears alone made the new ministry seem like an impossible endeavor. But keeping my eyes on Jesus, who knew all my fears, helped me get out of the boat.

To date, I have not attempted to walk on water. But I did start the ministry, which still thrives today.

Walking on water requires three things: a little fear, stepping out of the boat, and keeping your eyes on Jesus. All three of us—Jack, Peter, and I—were willing to step out. We didn't do it carelessly, but with confidence knowing that keeping our eyes on Jesus would make us stay afloat. When you face your fear and keep your eyes on Jesus, there's a pretty good chance you might walk on water.

CHILDLIKE FAITH ENCOURAGES US TO PURSUE WHAT WE LOVE

It was April of Jack's senior year of high school. Up to this point, Jack had not secured a summer job, and I was getting panicky. Although I greatly love my son, the thought of him lounging around all summer made me anxious. I kept suggesting job opportunities like the hardware store, the dry cleaners, or lawn mowing, but nothing seemed to light a fire under him.

One day we sat down to have a heart-to-heart talk about what his summer job aspirations were. "I want to work with kids." Okay, now we were getting somewhere! So Jack began applying at places where he would work with kids—the YMCA and area parks and recreation departments. Within the month, Jack was offered three jobs and accepted two—one coaching T-ball and the other, supervising kids at a day camp.

The work was much harder than Jack ever dreamed. All day long, kids climbed over every part of his body. Girls loved him because he would give them piggyback rides. Boys loved him because he could throw a ball. After day camp, he would go home to change clothes and grab his baseball gear. Then he'd drive to the ball fields and coach 5-year-olds in T-ball.

He loved those summer jobs. Working with the kids was rewarding, even if he didn't have much of a social life that summer. The kids wore him out, but Jack learned more about life, leadership, and fun because he stuck to his guns and pursued a job he loved.

PURSUE JESUS

Maybe at the time he didn't realize he was pursuing what he loved, but Nicodemus was curious. That curiosity led him to Jesus in the middle of the night.

Nicodemus was a member of the Jewish ruling council called the Pharisees. They opposed Jesus' claims that he was the Messiah. But Nicodemus wanted to know the truth. He wanted to know if Jesus really was who he said he was. So he visited Jesus.

They talked about a lot of things. During the conversation, Jesus shared with Nicodemus some of the most familiar words in the Bible: "For God so loved the world that he gave his one and only Son that whoever believes in Him shall not perish but have eternal life" (John 3:16). Most likely, Nicodemus could not fully grasp all Jesus was saying to him. Yet, these were the most amazing words Nicodemus had ever heard.

In the final account of Nicodemus, we see that he followed Jesus to his death. John 19:39 tells us "Nicodemus, the man who earlier had visited Jesus at night, brought a mixture of myrrh and aloes." Along with Joseph of Arimathea (who the Bible says was a disciple of Jesus), Nicodemus asked the Roman officials if they could take Jesus' body from the cross and prepare it for burial. Together, they wrapped his body with cloths and spices so he would have a burial in accordance with Jewish customs.

The contrast between the first and second accounts of Nicodemus is significant. The first time we learn about Nicodemus, he pursues Jesus secretly at night to learn the truth about him. The second time we hear about him, he pursues Jesus in the daylight and with extravagance. (Nicodemus provided an extravagant amount of spices for Jesus' burial.) The first visit was out of curiosity; the second was out of love.

We never hear of Nicodemus again in scripture. God tells us everything he wants us to know about Nicodemus in these two beautiful accounts. Nicodemus pursued what he loved. Then he pursued it (him) all the way to the cross. We are all like Nicodemus. Each of us must pursue Jesus, hear his truths, and then either believe or not.

Pursuing what you love will change your life, especially if that love is Jesus. It may change your direction, make you more aware, or it could take you to new places.

The Psalmist says, "Delight yourself in the Lord, and he will give you the desires of your heart" (Psalm 37:4). God knows what you love. Pursue it.

CHILDLIKE FAITH ASKS GOD
AND THEN BECOMES AMAZED

One day, fourteen-year-old Jack came home from baseball practice and said, "Coach has a potty mouth." This made me sad because he was Jack's favorite baseball coach. According to Jack, Coach said bad words—a lot.

A few days after our conversation about the cussing coach, our family was in church. During our pastor's sermon, he used an interesting verse. Even though it was not related to bad language, the pastor had us look up Ephesians 4:29, which says, "Do not let any unwholesome talk come out of your mouths, but only what is helpful for building others up according to their needs, that it may benefit those who listen." That afternoon Jack and I decided to commit that verse to prayer regarding Coach.

We began praying that verse on Monday morning before school. In fact, we prayed Ephesians 4:29 all week. On Friday afternoon, Jack walked in the back door with a huge grin on his face. "Guess what? You're never going to believe this."

He went on to tell me about how Coach had called a team meeting after practice. He apologized to the boys for using such strong language. He wanted to clean up his words, and asked the team to hold him accountable. My mouth dropped open in amazement. That prayer thing about asking God had actually worked!

Sometimes we moms say things just because we are supposed to say them. This is true about prayer. We teach our children to ask and to give our supplications to God. But do we really believe he is going to respond and answer our prayers? At most, we wish—or hope he will.

To be perfectly honest, I think I was more amazed at the outcome of our prayer for the cussing coach than Jack was. When it was all said and done, he was excited that God had answered our prayers, but he never really doubted. Instead, he demonstrated his childlike faith by trusting God with the outcome. I, on the other hand, was reminded that asking God is a great privilege and not just wishful thinking. This sweet experience helped me remember that asking God and then trusting him with childlike faith often leads to amazement.

A FATHER ASKS FOR HEALING

In the book of Luke, there is a story about a man whose son was possessed by an evil spirit. The man told Jesus, "A spirit seizes him... It scarcely ever leaves him and is destroying him" (Luke 9:39). Jesus asked the man to bring his son to him. The Bible says, "Even while the boy was coming, the demon threw him to the ground in a convulsion. But Jesus rebuked the evil spirit and healed the boy" (Luke 9:42). The Bible says the people who witnessed the healing were amazed at the greatness of God.

There are at least two common threads in the stories about Jack's coach and the father of the demon-possessed son. First, both Jack and the father asked God to do something for them. The Bible instructs us to ask God: "Ask and it will be given to you..." When Jesus teaches on prayer, he asks, "Which of you fathers, if your son asks for a fish, will give him a snake instead? If you, then... know how to give good gifts to your children, how much more will your Father in heaven give the Holy Spirit to those who ask Him?" (Luke 11:11-13). God wants us to ask and he wants to give to those who ask. Sometimes we just don't ask, and the answer is waiting. Just ask.

The second common thread is each was amazed when God answered his request. Jack and I were amazed at God's answer to our prayer about Coach. Likewise, the people were amazed at Jesus' healing of the demon-possessed boy. The word "amazed" is used forty-two times in the Bible. Twenty-nine of those refer to the work of Jesus. Jesus does amazing things.

The moment we realize God is intersecting our lives should be an amazing thing. Discovering the Sovereign of the universe cares about the matters of our lives hopefully puts us in a place of wonder. Yet all too often, we ask and then move on with our business with little remembrance of the asking. If we ask and then truly watch with expectation for an answer, God just might give us an opportunity to be wowed. God's answered prayers and our acknowledgment are a perfect opportunity for faith to grow in immeasurable ways.

Amazement reminds us to be simple and elemental. Simple in that even the smallest things are important to God and worth recognizing. And elemental in that God loves us as children and values us deeply. Think of what God is willing to do—just for you or just for me—how can we help but be amazed? So, here's the challenge: Just ask, recognize God's hand in it, and then be amazed.

PRAYING FOR THE LESSONS TO CONTINUE

Jack is now grown and living on his own. I'm grateful to him for all the lessons about faith he's taught me. I'm thankful that through *his* faith journey, I was sometimes able to become like a child, too.

The other day, he called to tell me he volunteered to coach a fourth-grade football team. Those lucky kids. Not only will they learn from a coach who has actually played the game (thank you to all the inexperienced dads who said yes because no one else would coach), but they will also receive life lessons from a person who is wise and relatable.

I bet Jack will also learn from those kids. I'm praying they will remind him often of the importance of becoming childlike again. I know from experience that learning from youngsters can be a powerful thing.

Becoming childlike happens in a variety of ways. Hurrying slowly helps define those things worth setting aside and those worth doing. It also encourages us to become intentional about savoring the moments. Facing our fears teaches us to keep our eyes on Jesus so when we are confronted with the scary things of life, we are able to trust the one who equips us to walk on water.

Pursuing Jesus changes the way we *look* at things in life while amazement teaches us to *see* God working in our lives. A childlike faith helps build our Jesus story because it expands our vision toward a God who desires to do mighty things for those who trust him.

By the way, you don't have to become a parent to learn about having childlike faith in Jesus. Jesus speaks to each individual about his love in the way it is most profound for that person. It is Jesus who is the perfect example of a son who loves his Father. Let him love you the way he loved Nicodemus and the way he loves Jack. His love can teach you amazing truths, but only if you let him.

IMMEASURABLY MORE MEANS

* Slow down and enjoy God's blessings.

* Look to Jesus instead of your fears because the power of Jesus working in you is greater than anything you will face in this world.

* Pursuing what you love can be wonderful when it involves Jesus.

* Be amazed at God.

YOUR JESUS STORY

* Share with someone or journal a time when you were entirely caught up in the moment. Describe your feelings.

* Are there things on your agenda keeping you from enjoying other things that may be more important (to you or to God)? List them. How can you intentionally slow yourself down so you can enjoy the moments?

* Is there something you consider risky, yet you feel God may be asking you to pursue?

* What kinds of things do you really love? How can you incorporate them into the everydayness of your life?

* When have you been amazed by God? What things will you do to allow yourself to be open to seeing God and letting him amaze you?

Dear Heavenly Father,

Sometimes life is so hard. However, I am the one who often makes it that way. I long for life to be simple and uncomplicated. You have given me a solution for this. You tell me to be childlike with my faith—to trust you, to be amazed by you, to pursue you, and not to hurry all the time. And when I do these things, you promise me I will rank in your kingdom because of my faithfulness. Help me, Father, to be more childlike so my faith is pleasing to you.

Amen.

 HOPE

When Life Is Not so Fun

We can rejoice, too, when we run into problems and trials,
for we know that they help us develop endurance.
And endurance develops strength of character,
and character strengthens our confident hope of salvation.
And this hope will not lead to disappointment.
For we know how dearly God loves us, because he has
given us the Holy Spirit to fill our hearts with his love.
ROMANS 5:3-5 (NLT)

Immeasurably more means Jesus gives you hope.

THE FEELING OF HOPELESSNESS

It was New Year's Eve. I had gone to bed early. While others were excited about the coming new year, I only felt anxiety. Looking to the next year, all I could see was a mountain I did not want to climb. There was no excitement—only dread.

Although I did not know exactly what to expect in the days ahead, I had a general idea. Dad had been struggling with memory loss for more than three years and had been noticeably declining over the past six months. My father was failing rapidly with Alzheimer's Disease. With my mother in poor health, I knew the responsibility of caring for my dad would rest with me.

We had barely made it through Christmas, but as we faced the new year, my father was crashing, mentally. And thus began my journey up the mountain.

There are times in life when you don't see tragedy coming. It can happen in an instant, and suddenly you are faced with a reality you did not expect. But there are other times when you know full well a challenge is coming. You can see it approaching and yet, you still don't know what to do. This is how it was for me.

One day in late December, I received a telephone call from my mother saying she could not control Dad. When I arrived at their home, he did not recognize me and I could see he was in another place and time. It was frightening. Soon after, he had another episode—much worse—and our only choice was to hospitalize him so he could be treated medically.

Mr. Wonderful is what we always called Dad. He was (and still is) wonderful. Always well-liked, my dad was shy and yet fun and funny. He loved adventure, music, and breaking rules. But mostly, Dad adored his wife and loved his three kids. My dad owned three campgrounds and spent much of his time outdoors. So to see this great outdoorsman reduced to an institutional life was painful.

It was a very sad time for me. My routine was the same every day. Each morning, I would drag myself out of bed and step into the shower. The shower became my crying room. And by crying, I mean the doubled-over, ugly, snot-down-your-face kind of crying. After the shower, I attempted to put myself together. Then I piddled around the house until it was time to visit Dad. Because visiting hours were short, I made sure I could spend the maximum amount of time with him.

Smiles occurred, but only infrequently. It's hard to lose someone while they are still alive. While others were moving on with life, enjoying the theater, good food, movies, great books, and baseball games, I had reduced my activities to spending time in hospitals and secured facilities with Dad. I was struggling to find any good thing in my circumstances. This was my new normal, and I felt like I was going to be stuck in this season of sadness forever.

A WOMAN NAMED BITTER

She had lost her husband and two grown sons. Living in a foreign land, she had no living children, no grandchildren, and no heirs. Life was as low as it gets. Her name was Naomi, but she asked to be called Mara, which means bitter.

Elimelech, Naomi's husband, moved his family to Moab because there was a famine in their homeland of Judah. While in Moab, Elimelech died, leaving Naomi with two sons and daughters-in-law. After ten years, the two sons also died.

Naomi was left alone in a foreign land with no way to support herself or her daughters-in-law. She discussed options with them. "Return home, my daughters. Why would you come with me? Am I going to have any more sons, who could become your husbands?" (Ruth 1:11)

Poor Naomi. She knew there was no way she could provide two more sons for her daughters-in-law. However, at this point, the women refused to leave her.

The word "hope" is first used in the Bible in this passage describing Naomi's sadness. Naomi says, *"Even if I thought there was still hope for me...."* Naomi was suggesting that there was nothing she could do for her daughters-in-law that would offer any hope and therefore, was releasing them from a life of bondage and responsibility to her.

With the famine over, Naomi saw no options other than to return home and see if a relative would take care of her. The three women began their journey back to Judah. Along the way, Naomi once again encouraged the young women to stay and marry someone from their own land. Naomi saw no hope for herself and certainly did not want to subject her daughters-in-law to a life of hopelessness, as well.

One stayed in Moab, but the other, Ruth, refused to leave Naomi. When Naomi and Ruth finally arrived in Judah, Naomi asked the townspeople to call her Mara because she was grieved the Lord had brought misfortune upon her.

Naomi was stuck because she couldn't see a solution to her problem. She felt hopeless because she could not see the future.

This is where hopelessness begins for any of us—when we cannot see the future. We get so bogged down by our current situation that we fail to recognize God might be doing something we cannot see. As Romans 5 suggests, these difficult times may just be a training ground for developing our endurance.

Often we say things like, "I hope I don't catch a cold" or "I hope it doesn't freeze tonight." This is actually *wishful thinking* rather than hope. We are wishing for something to happen but have no guarantee that it will. We want to be released from the difficult things and seek relief by asking for earthly blessings. We want our pain to go away.

Hope is so much more than wishful thinking.

Biblical hope is defined as "a certain expectancy." Unlike wishful thinking—where something may or may not come true—biblical hope is a confident assurance of knowing when God promises something, it is certain to happen.

Exactly what does God promise? Well, for one thing, he does *not* promise a trouble-free life. In fact, in John 16:33, Jesus guarantees we will have challenges: "In this world you will have trouble." Jesus is fully aware of the struggles we face. He knows that sometimes life seems hopeless.

But, Jesus does not leave us without hope. In the second part of the very same verse, he promises: "But take heart! I have overcome the world" (John 16:33). Jesus promises victory!

This explains why we can rejoice in our sufferings as Romans 5:3 suggests. Even though troubles will come, Jesus has overcome everything this world will throw our way. He may not eliminate the difficult circumstances, but he promises to join us during the times of troubles so we may eventually see a victory.

So if you are facing something where you cannot see a positive outcome, hang on. Don't give up. Jesus knows your struggles.

The victory Jesus promises may not be immediate. In fact, it may not occur while we are on earth. But we can know, without a shadow of a doubt, our hope will not disappoint because God said it won't.

On New Year's Day, I felt hopeless because I was wishing for my circumstances to change so I would feel better. My trial was bigger than I wanted to face. But God had given me a reason to be hopeful.

Instead of allowing myself to be stuck in my misfortune of that day, I could choose to look to him and remember his good promises to me. Through all of my care-taking of my father, God was teaching me to hang on. Soon I would discover the great lesson of endurance, which comes from the assurance of hope.

HOPEFUL

The clouds blocked my view of the mountain I was facing. Not knowing is always a challenge. The unknown is not easy. I forged ahead on my "Dad journey" anyway. I really had no choice. Truthfully, I was often overwhelmed. Emotionally, I was a mess.

Going to the hospital to see Dad was a daily drudgery. I was only allowed to visit at certain times of the day, privacy was nonexistent, and activities were a challenge. The patients all had difficult problems, and each one I encountered was a little odd.

However, God promised he would be with me, even at the hospital "When you pass through the waters, I will be

with you and when you pass through the rivers, they will not
sweep over you.

> *When you walk through the fire,*
> *you will not be burned,*
> *the flames will not set you ablaze.*
> ISAIAH 43:2

My endurance lesson was teaching me that God would join
me in the most unusual places. I wanted to focus on him, not
my circumstances. I asked God to give me a visible reminder
of his presence every day. I needed so badly to see him working in real ways I could identify.

One day while at the hospital, my dad and I were sitting
on his bed looking at photos. A woman walked by his room
and asked if she could look at the pictures with us. She sat
down next to me and said, "Hi, I'm Tracy."

As we visited, I learned Tracy was a housekeeper in another
department. Her shift ended at three o'clock each day and
her husband, who also worked at the hospital, didn't get off
until three thirty. Tracy thought the seniors needed a little
more attention, so instead of going to the break room, she
spent her extra thirty minutes with them.

We had a lovely conversation about our families but mostly
about Dad. At three thirty, Tracy stood to leave. As she walked
out the door, she turned to me and said, "I hope it's okay with
you, but today, I held your dad's hands and prayed with him."

Sweet Tracy the housekeeper was my visible reminder
of God. Through her, I was reminded that God stays with

me, even in the hospital. This encounter made me hopeful. I learned that sometimes the presence of God will appear in the most unexpected ways to help me keep looking to him. Today it appeared in the form of a housekeeper.

I am a person of spiritual discipline. I like reading my Bible. Prayer is part of each day. Praise songs and hymns regularly play on my car radio. But during this season of sadness, I found it difficult to pursue God in my normal ways. Many days, my Bible went untouched. Button number two, the country music station, became the most listened-to music in my car.

Yet, I never felt closer to God. I felt his presence everywhere. God hadn't removed the hard circumstances from my life. Instead, he joined in. Looking to his promises instead of my circumstances was helping me develop my endurance and strengthen my character.

What are some of those promises God made to me?

* He promised to hear my prayers: "This is the confidence we have in approaching God: that if we ask anything according to his will, he hears us" (1 John 5:14).

* He promised to be faithful to me: "God is faithful, who has called you into fellowship with his Son, Jesus Christ our Lord."

* He promised to be with me no matter what: "So do not fear, for I am with you" (Isaiah 41:10).

* He promised to strengthen me: "I will strengthen you and help you" (Isaiah 41:10).

Claiming his promises during these challenging times gave me the strength to move forward. These promises taught me

I was not without hope. I held on to them because they were my lifeline.

HOPE FOR NAOMI

We cannot see the things God can see.

* We see emptiness and failure; he sees fullness and a future.

* We see tragedy; he sees victory.

* We see storms; he sees us through the storms.

God was not expecting Naomi to journey through life alone. He promised to be with her as she passed through the waters. Although she couldn't see it, God had great plans for Naomi and her family. Through Boaz, a relative—a redeemer—God's presence and his plan became known to Naomi.

The name Boaz means "in him is strength." He was a relative of Elimelech and offered a special kind of hope because he was known as a "kinsman-redeemer." In the Bible, the kinsman-redeemer was a near relative who was responsible for protecting the interests of needy members of the extended family.

According to Jewish law, Israelites could sell themselves, their families, or their lands in cases of poverty. A near relative had the first option, by law, to buy any land being sold, thus allowing it to be kept within the clan. In the Bible, the kinsman-redeemer relationship was established so the land could remain in the family and individuals in the clan would be protected.

It just so happened Naomi's daughter-in-law, Ruth, went to Boaz's field to gather grain. The poor were allowed to follow behind the field workers and pick up any leftover grain. Boaz noticed Ruth. Because of Ruth's kindness to her mother-in-law, Boaz showed favor to her. When Ruth returned from the fields, she told Naomi about the generosity of Boaz. Hope began to bubble up in Naomi. She knew the Lord had been faithful by bringing Boaz into their lives.

I cried every time I left the hospital. The security person handed me a tissue each day on the way out. Then he nodded and smiled at me. Once again, God joined me. This time it was through a simple nod and a sweet smile of a security person assuring me I had made it through another visit. I wished so badly I could've smiled back.

Weeks passed and the day finally came to move Dad to a permanent nursing home. On his last day in the hospital, I stepped through the locked doors and spoke to the security person with a hopeful feeling. "Look at me! I don't need a tissue today." I had survived the hospital experience.

In order to keep my focus on God instead of my troubles, I had asked him to join me in my journey. He chose to do this through a housekeeper and a security person. Through them, he reminded me that my circumstances weren't hopeless.

My trials did not end the day Dad left the hospital. But through this experience, God had revealed himself and given me the endurance to make it through. He also showed me how this endurance was strengthening my character. I was becoming a person of confident hope.

NOT ONLY RESCUED, BUT RESTORED

God had a plan of rescue for Naomi and Ruth through Boaz. The sweetest part of this story is that God did not stop at rescue. He did more. "So Boaz took Ruth and she became his wife. Then he went to her, and the Lord enabled her to conceive, and she gave birth to a son" (Ruth 4:13). Naomi finally had a grandchild! Only months before, she was an empty, bitter, and hopeless woman. Her God, who never left her and who always had a plan for her future, restored her with joy and hope.

"They named him Obed. He was the father of Jesse and the grandfather of David" (Ruth 4:17). Naomi's great-great grandchild would one day become a king. And through the line of this king, the Savior of the whole world would be born. His name would be Jesus. The woman who was hopeless became a representative of never-ending hope.

The time in the nursing home was sad but sweet. My dad never knew who I was after the hospital. But his wonderful personality stayed intact. He was a staff favorite. The tears came less often, although I knew the end was near.

Less than a year later, my dad passed away. Not long after Dad was gone, my niece, Julie, came over to my house for a visit. She was bubbly and full of life, and it was refreshing to be around her. "My word for the year is 'illuminate,'" she said to me.

"What's a word for the year?"

"I claim a word that I try to live into each year."

"I want a word."

After she left, I sat down in my little chair in the kitchen. I didn't have to think long about my word. I already knew it even before she told me about a word for the year.

My word was "smile."

After the last year, smiling no longer came naturally. I had to practice. And practice, I did. I smiled in the bathroom mirror. I smiled at people in the car next to me at the stoplight. I smiled at the grocery clerk.

Before long, smiling came naturally again.

And that's when it hit me. Romans 5:3-5 was true. I could rejoice. Yes, the trial was hard, but God had seen me through it. God had taught me that wishful thinking was not enough. Endurance. Strength of character. Confident hope. God's love. These were the things that gave me reason to rejoice.

Claiming the word "smile" showed me that perhaps on another day, my smile may just be enough to share God's hope with someone else. Perhaps I can become someone's representative of hope.

HOPE-FILLED

My dad loved to build things. He built three campgrounds. He built our family home.

But as I grew older, I realized houses weren't the only things Dad was skilled at building. He was most interested in helping build lives. We always had house guests while I was growing up. Sometimes it was a troubled child of one of my parents' friends. Other times, it was someone who just needed a place to stay for awhile.

My dad hired many employees over the years, but his employees consisted of people who wouldn't be able to get jobs otherwise. He hired troubled youth, people with jail records, and the uneducated; just about anyone who needed a job. My dad gave these people dignity when no one else saw value in them. I personally had a front row seat in watching individuals go from hopeless to hope-filled.

When I think about it, my whole life represents a life my dad helped build. Fred was an amazing inspiration, role model, and caring dad. His life was far from easy. I remember on especially difficult days, Dad would say, "God is never going to give me more today than what he and I can handle together."

He never held on to earthly things too tightly because he valued an eternal perspective. As a man of hope, my dad never doubted his future. His confidence assured me death was not the end, but a beginning. Perhaps his biggest contribution to my life was his model of hope. He taught me that trials shape our character and prepare us for heaven.

Isn't it interesting that my ultimate endurance lesson was given to me by my dad as he struggled with Alzheimer's? I kind of feel like my earthly father and heavenly father partnered to teach me that I can rejoice in my trials because suffering produces hope. Through it all, I discovered hope does not disappoint.

My father went to be with Jesus on January 20, 2011. Although he is not physically present now, his spirit lives on through me and the lives of many others. My earthly father modeled hope. My Heavenly Father gives hope.

IMMEASURABLY MORE MEANS

* God will show you visible reminders of him if you ask him.

* When you focus on God instead of your circumstances, it transforms you from feeling hopeless to becoming hopeful.

* Hope never disappoints because God loves you, and he is the source of your hope.

* Troubles will not end on this earth, but God promises a trouble-free eternity.

YOUR JESUS STORY

* Read Isaiah 43:1-4

⇒ What does it mean to you that God promises to be with you when you pass through the waters, the rivers, and fire?

⇒ Recall a time when you passed through waters or fire. Did you feel God's presence? If you did, how did that make you feel? If you did not, how could this promise help you in future struggles?

* Do you believe God hears your prayers? If you do, why not ask him to be a visible presence in your life today?

❋ If you are in a time of despair, how can you let other Christian women walk with you?

SOME OF THE PROMISES MADE (AND KEPT) BY GOD

Looking to God and his promises gives us hope. God is both a promise maker and a promise keeper. His Word, the Bible, is a book of promises. Some scholars say there are more than 5,000 promises made in the Bible, which means there are also more than 5,000 promises *kept* in the Bible. Because of hope, we can know with a certain expectancy God and his promises are true. This not only makes us hopeful, but more importantly, hope-filled.

He is always with you.

For the Lord your God will be
with you wherever you go.
JOSHUA 1:9

He hears your prayers.

Evening, morning and at noon,
I will pray and He shall hear my voice.
PSALM 55:7

He delivers you from fear.

I sought the Lord, and He heard me,
and delivered me from all my fears.
PSALM 34:4

He will forgive you.

If we confess our sins, He is faithful and just
to forgive us our sins and to cleanse us
from all unrighteousness.
1 JOHN 1:9

He is faithful.

Let us hold fast the confession of our hope
without wavering, for He who promised is faithful.
HEBREWS 10:23

He will never quit loving you.

I have loved you with an everlasting love.
JEREMIAH 31:3

Our kind and Heavenly Father,

Without you, I am hopeless. With you, I am hope-filled. The kindness of your hope helps me keep eternity in perspective. I know this earth life matters, Lord. But without you it would be meaningless. Help me, Father, to always look to you—especially when I'm troubled. Give me compassion, Jesus, so that I may be your hands and feet when others are having a difficult time seeing you. Thank you, Lord, that you are with me no matter the circumstances.

Amen.

chapter seven

✳ WHOLEHEARTED ✳

The Journey of a Lifetime

*Serve wholeheartedly, as if you were
serving the Lord, not people.*
EPHESIANS 6:7

**Immeasurably more means
Jesus makes your life wild and wonderful.**

I remember the day. It was the day I knew I loved Steve and he was my forever man.

We were in college. He was walking me from his fraternity house to my apartment. We stopped at my mailbox to pick up my mail. (People still mailed things via the postal service in the 1980s). We were laughing and being silly. It was just one of those joyous days.

I inserted the key to unlock the box when Steve stopped me. He looked me in the eyes and very seriously said, "Susan, when I am with you, I am better. You just make me better." I'm pretty sure I had already told Steve I loved him several times before. But in that moment, I knew, without a shadow of a doubt, I was *in love* with him. I knew his words were true because the same was true for me. Steve made me better too.

When I was thirteen I had an experience with Jesus similar to the one that occurred at the mailbox with Steve. Even though I was nine when I asked Jesus to come live in my heart, it wouldn't be until four years later that I knew I loved Jesus wholeheartedly.

Our family was taking a vacation in our RV. My sister and I were in the very back and as we bumped down the highway, I asked my sister, "Mary, what does it really mean for Jesus to live in my heart?" My sister is four years older than me and I believed she knew the answer to all things.

"It means that when you were nine, you asked Jesus to be your Savior so you could live a full life with him here on earth and one day be reunited with him in heaven." My sister went on to say something that has always stuck with me. "But, Susan, to really be in love with Jesus and to follow him, he must not only be your Savior, but he must be sovereign in your life. Everything you do and say must be filtered through him because he loves you and knows what is best for you. This is how you live a long and full life with him."

All these years later, Jesus is still both a savior to me and sovereign over me. Because of this, I believe Jesus makes me better. Following and trusting Jesus makes me a better wife, mom, sister, and friend. Hanging out with Jesus helps me look more like him. And I think this makes me a better Susan.

Not only does Jesus make me better, he promises to travel with me and help me on life's journey. When I'm afraid, he is the one I look to. When I feel alone, he is my constant companion. When I feel unloved, Jesus reminds me I'm his first love. Because Jesus is all these things to me and more, I want to follow him—not just sort of but wholeheartedly.

THE TIME OF MY LIFE

One day, my husband came home from work and mentioned he had a business meeting in Orlando. He wondered if Jack (who was three) and I wanted to go to Disney World with him. Disney with our three-year-old? Of course I wanted to go. It was a dream come true!

When I was a child, my parents took me to Disney so I knew how magical the place was. I had dreamed of the day when I could take my own child. Twenty years later, that dream was finally coming true. I was returning to Disney World. Only this time I was taking my little boy with me.

As if that wasn't enough, my parents were already in Florida and happily agreed to meet us there. My four favorite people in the world were visiting the happiest place in the world with me! It was too good to be true. I told everybody about our upcoming adventure to the Magic Kingdom.

Time crept by. After weeks of planning, the day finally arrived for our big trip. Bags were packed. Plane tickets were secured. We were off to Disney World.

Twenty years had passed since my first visit to Disney. My excitement about returning intensified because I knew a wonderful experience was waiting. I hoped my excitement wasn't exaggerated. Would Disney meet my expectations? Was it still all I had dreamed it would be?

We arrived to perfect weather in beautiful Florida. Flowers bloomed everywhere. Everything was just as great as I remembered. After checking into the hotel, we immediately set out for the park.

Stepping off the monorail (the happy train that takes you from your hotel to the park), I couldn't quit grinning. Life was so big at that moment. After all these years, I was returning to the happiest place on earth. Practically breathless, I looked to my dad and said, "I'm having the time of my life, and we haven't even done anything yet!"

There was a man in the Bible who was given the chance to visit the Promised Land. Like my initial Disney experience, he saw firsthand how magnificent the place was. He walked it with his own feet and saw it with his own eyes. However, after visiting the Promised Land, it was forty years before he would return.

A DIFFERENT SPIRIT

He was born into slavery.

He was part of the tribe of Judah.

He was one of twelve spies.

He wanted to take possession of the Promised Land.

He followed the Lord wholeheartedly.

His name was Caleb.

In Numbers 13, the Lord instructed Moses to send some men to explore the land of Canaan. Canaan was also called the Promised Land because God promised to give it to the Israelites. Moses selected twelve men—one from each tribe of Israel—to investigate all aspects of the land—the food, the people, the cities, everything. After forty days of exploring the food, people, cities and anything else, they returned with news about their discoveries.

Their report came with mixed reviews. Of the twelve men, only two—Caleb and Joshua—had the courage to lead the Israelites into the Promised Land. The other ten wavered. They feared the people living in the land. This lack of trust made God angry. As a result, God vowed that not one Israelite man who left Egypt as a slave would see the Promised Land. So instead of taking the land God had already given them, the Israelites roamed the desert for forty years.

Only Caleb and Joshua from the original group would be allowed to eventually enter the land. After his disappointment with the Israelites, God specifically explains why Caleb would return to the Promised Land:

> "...because my servant Caleb has a **different spirit**
> and follows me **wholeheartedly**,
> I will bring him into the land he went to."
> NUMBERS 14:24a

Caleb had a different spirit. Unlike the ten who wavered, Caleb remembered God's faithfulness from the past and, as a result, trusted him with the future. In his short lifetime, Caleb had already seen God do amazing things.

* He experienced his own death passed over by his promise-keeping God.

* He walked into freedom as God delivered his people from slavery in Egypt.

* He witnessed a miracle when God parted the sea that brought his family and all the Israelites into safety.

* He ate manna, the heavenly bread provided by God when his people were starving in the desert.

Trusting God even when the stakes were high gave Caleb a different spirit.

Not only did Caleb trust God to lead his people into conflict and give them the victory, he was also certain of God's ability. Hear the passion in Caleb's voice when he addresses the Israelite community: "We should go up and take possession of the land for we can certainly do it" (Numbers 13:30). What gave Caleb a different spirit? He knew life with God was so much better than life without him.

LOOK TO GOD IN THE MIDST OF THE HAZARDS

Entering the Promised Land included many hazards. The people who lived there were big and scary. However, Caleb was willing to face the hazards because God had already promised the Israelites the land regardless of the circumstances they faced. All they needed to do was to go and take it.

Two different reports were given by the men who explored the Promised Land—those who wavered and Caleb. Caleb saw the hazard from a different perspective than the other ten. To see the difference in each perspective, read the following passages and circle every time the "*Lord*" is used:

The report given by the ten who wavered:

They reported to… the whole assembly and showed them the fruit of the land. They gave Moses this account: "We went into the land to which you sent us and it does flow with milk and honey!… But the people who live there are powerful, and the cities are fortified and very large…. We can't attack those people; they are stronger than we are" (Numbers 13:26-31 paraphrased).

The report given by Caleb and Joshua:

Caleb said to the entire assembly, "The land we passed through is exceedingly good. If the LORD is pleased with us, He (LORD) will lead us into that land… and (the LORD) will give it to us. The LORD is with us" Numbers 14:7-9 paraphrased).

Do you see what's missing in the first report? The ten didn't even mention the Lord. They only saw the giants. Caleb saw the giants, too. But the difference between the ten who wavered and Caleb was when the ten looked at the giants, they only saw an obstacle. When Caleb looked at the giants, he saw the Lord's power. Caleb knew the challenge would be great. But he knew God was greater. Even though the journey would most likely be long, uncertain, and difficult, Caleb trusted God would go with them.

Obstacles have a way of blocking our vision because we have a hard time seeing past them. We focus more on the problem, which prevents us from fathoming a solution. Our limited vision keeps us from seeing how God might navigate us through a difficult time.

When we, like Caleb, look to our trustworthy God instead of the obstacle, we are choosing to gaze towards our source for a solution rather than focusing on the problem itself. God may not give us an immediate answer or solve all of our problems, but the certainty of knowing he goes with us gives us strength to cope.

WHEN GOD MADE A PROMISE

Years ago, God made a promise to me. "Susan, I know the plans I have for you, plans to prosper you and not to harm you, plans to give you a hope and a future" (Jeremiah 29:11). I trusted God with this promise. But a few years after that, I was tested to see how much I really believed it.

The obstacle I faced was huge. I couldn't imagine how God was going to provide a more perfect job for me than the one I had created for myself as training director. It was a dream job. I had just graduated with a master's degree in adult education and training was my passion. Working in sales for a large urban hotel, I desired to create a spectacular training department for our hotel.

With a new degree in hand, I proposed to my boss the creation of a part-time position allowing me to teach and train the hotel employees. At the time, I was four months pregnant. Big changes were about to happen in my life. I knew the time-consuming schedule of my current full-time job would not be possible as a new mother. A part-time position in training seemed perfect.

Weeks passed after I submitted my proposal and I was called into my boss's office. He gave me a thumbs-up. The position had been approved.

However, the evening before my boss called me into his office, my husband came home from work and excitedly told me he had been given a promotion. We were moving from Kansas City to Chicago. The part-time training position ended before it even started. It's kind of amazing how this one event changed the trajectory of my life.

When I was in college, I had always dreamed of living in a big city with a wonderful job. Funny, I had half of the dream with this sudden change. I was moving to a big city but my job would be taking care of a baby. I never dreamed I would be a stay-at-home mom.

The first few months were a bit challenging. With my husband new to a career, he spent a good bit of time working. I didn't know anyone in my new town or anything about being a mother. Little did I know, God's good plans for my life were just getting started in Chicago.

He knew if I had accepted the hotel training job back in Kansas City, I would have never worked only part-time. He knew what was best for me (at the time) was to step away from that opportunity and become a stay-at-home mom. There was no choice but to put the working world on hold and enjoy some time with my baby. And that's exactly what I did.

Over the years, I've come to realize when we are stripped down, God can do some of his best work. What I mean by this is when we can't see a direction or are confused about our future, this is the time when God can do immeasurably more than we ever imagined. If we only submit, his dreams for us can be so much greater than anything we could have dreamed for ourselves.

My passion for teaching and training didn't diminish. Eventually, God allowed me to ease into a part-time teaching job at the local college. Then, we moved again. Soon after, God opened a door for me to start my own training company. This was brilliant on God's part because my part-time company went with me as we moved three more times. God's plans for me were marching forward but he wasn't nearly finished with me and my vocation.

A friend was starting an evangelism ministry and asked me to become one of her national trainers. After several years of training in my own small business, God was opening a door for me to train for him! My passion for training along with my experience allowed me to work in God's business.

As I look back, I'm awed at how God kept his promise to prosper me. For more than the past twenty years, I have had the remarkable opportunity to teach and train thousands of women all over the country. My passion in training never changed. God knew that. What seemed to be an obstacle earlier in life was really just a training ground for the bigger things God had in mind for me.

IN THE DESERT

God promised Caleb he would one day enter the Promised Land, but he didn't go immediately. He lived in the desert for forty years. Even though Caleb trusted God, he still paid the price for the rest of the Israelite's unbelief. "For forty years—one for each of the forty days you explored the land—you will suffer for your sins" (Numbers 14:34). Caleb, by no fault of his own, waited until the punishment had been served by all before he entered the Promised Land.

Not only would Caleb wait, he would also see all his friends die in the desert. "Not one of the men who saw my glory and the miraculous signs I performed in Egypt and in the desert but who disobeyed me… will never see the land I promised" (Numbers 14:22-23). Surely Caleb's heart broke as he watched his friends and their families slowly die off. His grief must have been overwhelming.

The Bible gives us no details about Caleb's time in the desert. He certainly could have played the victim during the forty years. But that does not seem to be the case. Through all the waiting and watching, Caleb's different spirit never took his eyes off God.

Perhaps this different spirit allowed Caleb to minister to his friends while they were in the desert. It's possible Caleb, who was in a desert himself, helped comfort those who were grieving and lost.

Waiting and watching are two of the most difficult aspects of the desert season. Waiting while everyone else seems to be enjoying life or at the very least, moving on, is a painful part of the journey. Waiting is like an obstacle. But we can choose where we will keep our gaze—on God or our circumstances.

Like Caleb, our different spirit becomes evident when we trust God even though we cannot see the clear answer. Dry seasons give us an opportunity to seek God in ways we would not otherwise find him. Ultimately, waiting and watching expands our faith.

Sometimes it seems like we suffer even though we have done nothing wrong. Feeling powerless while we're struggling seems unfair. Caleb's story reminds us following God does not exempt us from the hardships of life. But we learn from Caleb that God walks with those who have a different spirit. He equips us to make it through. And sometimes, even though we are in a desert ourselves, God may ask us to help others walk the journey.

MY FRIEND PAT

My friend Pat just celebrated her 90th birthday. She attends a Bible study I teach. She is a retired schoolteacher and pastor's wife. Her unique gift is making everyone feel special. I like to think I'm Pat's favorite. But the truth is Pat makes every woman in our Bible study feel like she's her favorite. I love Pat for many reasons, but there are two particular reasons she is so special to me.

Pat reminds me of Caleb: She has a different spirit and lives wholeheartedly.

One day after teaching Bible study, Pat approached me and asked what was wrong. I was surprised. I didn't think I had said anything during class to warrant her asking. However, her perception was correct. There was something wrong. Weeks before, I had stepped away from a long-term ministry involvement and was feeling like I was stuck in a desert. In all the previous years of ministry, God had been very clear about my next steps. I was feeling lost and couldn't see what was next for me. I wondered if he was retiring me.

I sat on a bench with Pat and cried. She was a great comfort. I'm not really sure what Pat *said* to me, but I will never forget what she *did* for me. She noticed my sadness and then followed up with a listening ear. My desert experience did not end that day with Pat on the bench. But her small act of encouragement provided a little push to keep me going.

Following Jesus gives all of us a different spirit. However, sometimes during the difficult seasons, we need a little help. Pat told me there was never a shortage of people who helped her during her desert seasons.

We all need someone like Pat who gives us a little push. This person may not be a forever friend, but just someone who notices and acts. It is important to seek out people like Pat in our own lives. Ask God to give you a Pat. Join a small group at your church where other women participate. But equally as important, be a Pat for someone else. Take the time to not only notice, but also show concern when someone is struggling. The truth is we couldn't live wholehearted lives if it wasn't for the accumulation of those like Pat who encourage us to keep trusting God.

LIVING WHOLEHEARTEDLY

I don't know anyone who lives life more wholeheartedly than Pat. Not only is she a caring and wise woman, she is a role model in the way she lives her very involved life. Pat says even though she is very busy, she only does things that matter and have a purpose. She sings in the choir (has for 70 years), tutors at an elementary school, attends a book club, participates in an investment club, and encourages people through her letter writing. She never misses my class unless she is visiting one of her children or grandchildren.

One day I asked Pat, "How do you do it? How do you live a wholehearted life?" She replied simply, "That's the way I am. I only have two speeds: stop and go." She went on to tell me, "I see all these people just wasting their lives by doing nothing."

According to Pat, if you see a problem, stop complaining and go and do something about it. Certainly, Pat has had challenges in her life. For example, I asked her how she coped when her husband traveled often as she was raising four young children. She said, "You just do what you have to do—every day."

Pat's secret to living a wholehearted life is trusting and following the Lord every step of the way. Regardless if she was teaching school, raising her children, or moving around the country, Pat always kept her eyes on God and trusted him with the details.

She takes no credit for her hard work. Every time I lovingly thank Pat for supporting me, she responds, "Pfff, I haven't done anything." But I know that's not true. I've seen many other lives helped and encouraged by her. Pat's very full life is a great reminder that focusing on God not only makes the journey meaningful, but is also the key to remaining strong along the way.

Forty years have passed. The time has come to enter the land God promised. Caleb is not only excited, he is ready. He reminds Joshua, who is now leader of the army, what God said: "The land on which your feet have walked will be your inheritance... because you have followed the Lord wholeheartedly" (Joshua 14:9).

By his own testimony, Caleb was as strong then as he was forty years before. He was as vigorous in battle as he was the first time God sent him into the land (Joshua 14:11). He was ready to go, ready to fight, and ready for his inheritance. And now, with the same passion and certainty, Caleb—with God's help—takes the land God promised him many years before.

Caleb never held back because he knew God's plans for him were greater than he ever could have dreamed. He knew the desert was only part of his journey. And now, he was entering into the Promised Land still following God wholeheartedly.

What do Caleb and Pat have in common? They both have a different spirit and follow God wholeheartedly. They looked to God rather than their obstacles. They didn't let the desert define them. They did things with certainty because they knew a life with God made them better.

SIXTH-GRADE BASKETBALL

Not long ago, I spent a week with my son in Birmingham, Alabama. He had just purchased a home, and I was there doing "mom stuff" with the move. On top of the move, Jack was coaching a sixth-grade basketball team, and they were playing their first game on Thursday. It had been a pretty full week, and I was tired. I knew Jack was tired too, so I rode over to the game to keep him company.

Truth be told, when Jack played sixth-grade basketball, I didn't really enjoy it. It was always cold walking into the gym. The gym was always stinky like a boys locker room. And usually, the games were not all that great. Very few sixth-grade stars make it into the NBA, if you know what I mean.

Anyway, as Jack and I got out of the car, I said to myself, "What was I thinking?" I was immediately transported back in time sixteen years ago. It was cold. The gymnasium was still stinky. The bleachers were no softer than they were in all those years ago. And now I was watching a bunch of boys I didn't even know play basketball.

The game began. It didn't take long to peg all the players. There was the crier—the poor kid who couldn't keep his emotions under control. There was the question-asker—the one who needed confirmation on everything. There was the athlete—the one boy who actually was good at basketball. It was pretty surprising. These were the same boys who played on my son's team all those years ago. Nothing had really changed. Only the names and faces were different.

I found myself smiling because as I looked around, I noticed the parents hadn't changed either. There was the coach-dad who sat right behind my son and "helped" call the plays. There was the yelling mom who coached her son from the top of the bleachers. There were the cool parents who everyone wanted to sit near. I couldn't help but wonder which parent was me all those years ago.

Before long, I was actually enjoying the game. Then one of the boys fouled out. He was frustrated and acted like any other sixth-grade boy who was disappointed. He came off the court and sat down in a huff. Then something pretty cool happened. I watched proudly as my son, the coach, encouraged, built up, and supported this boy. I watched this sixth-grader transform from frustrated to calm because his coach walked him through his disappointment.

At that moment, I so badly wanted to turn around and tell each parent sitting in the bleachers, "It's going to be okay.

You won't be stuck in sixth-grade basketball forever." I wanted to say, "I've seen the Promised Land, and it ain't here!" I wanted to tell them that one day their young son will grow up and maybe become the encouraging coach of a sixth-grade basketball team.

And that is when it struck me. I realized I was on the other side of this part of the journey. And the other side is good. My life is good.

I never dreamed I'd be sitting in a gym at this stage in my life. I had always envisioned myself in a corporate board-room. But the gym? What I was seeing was good. And God's plans were good.

My journey is far from over, but trusting God and following him helps me live wholeheartedly. This kind of living only makes my life better.

WHOLEHEARTEDLY

Caleb saw the Promised Land, waited in the desert forty years, then returned—all while living wholeheartedly. In a sense, we too, have seen the Promised Land. Jesus, himself, is our Promised Land. The day we say yes to him is the day our story begins.

Following Jesus wholeheartedly does not mean everything in life turns out perfectly. Far from it. Life is hard. Craziness surrounds us in both people and circumstances. Rarely do things turn out as we plan. But life is a journey. Within the big journey are a bunch of mini-journeys. You may be at the beginning, in the middle, or have made it to the other side. And no one else can take your journey for you—it is yours alone.

Your relationship with Jesus tells your story of how you do the journey. You can choose to trust him and follow him wholeheartedly, even if life does not turn out as you planned.

With Jesus, life is so much more—immeasurably more.

You can know this is true because here's what he says to you: "My purpose is to give (you) a rich and satisfying life" (John 10:10). He wants you to wake up each morning and know he's joining you in all the moments of your day.

This is what makes life wild and wonderful: Seeing your story unfold as you live each day with Jesus.

IMMEASURABLY MORE MEANS

* Jesus wants to be both Savior and sovereign in your life.

* Remembering God's past faithfulness helps find comfort in the future.

* Trusting God's promises keeps your eyes on God instead of your circumstances.

* Noticing and acting helps others live wholehearted lives.

* God will not keep you in the desert forever.

* A wholehearted life is the accumulation of experiences masterfully woven together by God.

YOUR JESUS STORY

* What are some promises God has made to you?

* When you were (are) in the desert, what do you think God might be teaching you?

* How do you celebrate when God has revealed a purpose for a particular journey?

* Maybe your Jesus story is not turning out as you planned. What are some unexpected blessings that have happened?

O Sovereign God,

You are the great one. You are the one who should be praised. You are the one who rescued me and saved me. I want to live my entire life with passion for you. You are the one who keeps me strong. You give me a different spirit. You make me better. I want to serve you wholeheartedly. I trust you with my life, Lord.

Amen.

✳ AMEN ✳

Amen.

Why do we say amen at the end of a prayer?

Is it a code word that means the prayer is over?

The word "amen" is defined as "so be it," "truly," "trust-worthy," and "faithful." So when we close a prayer with amen, we are agreeing with the truth of what was said. For example, if I pray, "Lord, you are good and faithful. Amen," what I mean is I agree and trust that God is good and faithful.

In the introduction of this book, we looked at the importance of the tiny word "yes." We learned God said yes through his son, Jesus, to every promise he made for us. We acknowledged saying yes to Jesus is the most important yes. And we discovered God's yes combined with our yes is the beginning of a wild and wonderful life with Jesus.

Second Corinthians 1:20 reminds us of one more important piece to experiencing a wild and wonderful life: It's the proclamation of "amen."

> *Whatever God has promised gets stamped*
> *with the Yes of Jesus. In him, this is what we*
> *preach and pray,* **the great Amen,**
> *God's Yes and our Yes together, gloriously evident.*

> *God affirms us, making us a sure thing*
> *in Christ, putting his Yes within us.*
> *By his Spirit he has stamped us with his eternal pledge—*
> *a sure beginning of what he is destined to complete.*
> 2 CORINTHIANS 1:20-22, THE MESSAGE

When you say "amen," you acknowledge that Jesus makes all his promises a reality. Your amen places a period at the end of all the truths you believe about him.

In this book, you explored a wild and wonderful life with Jesus. You examined seven truths to make your Jesus story immeasurably more than you imagined. As you read and reflect, consider saying your amen to each truth below:

* I believe Jesus wants to be my best friend. Amen.

* I believe Jesus makes me become the best version of myself. Amen.

* I believe Jesus showed his greatest love for me by giving himself. Amen.

* I believe Jesus longs for me to know him through the riches of his glorious words, the Bible. Amen.

* I believe a childlike faith helps me trust Jesus more. Amen.

* I believe Jesus offers hope even when I feel hopeless. Amen.

* I believe Jesus wants me to live wholeheartedly. Amen.

Jesus does not want us to live defeated, bland, and purposeless lives. A wild and wonderful life with him as our friend, our hope, our life, and our love is the prescription for a rich, satisfying, and wholehearted life. Please, go live your Jesus story. Let his spark ignite in you so when it's all said and done, you will say, "Wow, what a ride!" Amen!

acknowledgments

In writing about my story, I realize many people have played a part—not only in this book, but also in my life. I am blessed to have family and friends who make my life both wild and wonderful. My mother, Olive, and father, Fred, gave me a sense of adventure and fun and encouraged me to live wildly. My sister, Mary, was an early role model in my faith journey and continues to be a source of wisdom in all things "life." My big brother, Jack, somehow dodged any mention in the stories of this book. However, he is an inspiration because of his ability to dream, and his gift of encouragement.

My Tuesday morning Bible study gals have endured years of my teaching and storytelling. Not only have they listened, critiqued, and supported me, but they also allowed me to try new teaching techniques and practice public speaking engagements with them. But more importantly, these gals are my friends and support group. This group of Bible study-loving ladies makes my life rich.

If it weren't for Susan Tolleson, my book coach, *A Wild & Wonderful Life* would still be sitting on a computer without a future. Her expertise helped organize my thoughts and words, while her encouragement kept me at it.

Thank you, Carly Robinson, for capturing artwork for the cover and throughout the book that artistically and so beautifully represents what I think a wild and wonderful life looks like.

I'm grateful to Sally Retz, Lori Krueger, Leslie Adams, Ruthie Anderson, Leslie McGowan, and Gina Keohan, who all helped me with the book writing process.

Thank you, Jack Bart Campbell, for saying just the right thing at just the right time when I wanted to quit writing. Thank you for seeing something in me that I couldn't see in myself. Thank you for becoming a young man who loves Jesus and his mama. People say that children are a gift from God. Thank you for being the gift that keeps on giving.

It's nice to be able to share a life with someone you not only *love* wholeheartedly, but also *like* immeasurably more! Steve, love of my life, thank you for riding along with me on all my adventures; especially this book.

Jesus, you are the story of my life. The great hymn says it best: "This is my story. This is my song, praising my savior, all the day long!"

about susan

Since the age of nine, Susan has had a wild and wonderful relationship with Jesus. Her involvement in women's ministries for the past twenty-plus years has allowed her to develop several women's ministry programs. Susan has trained thousands of women on leadership, volunteerism, and program development. She is founder of More Than You Imagine Ministries and co-author of Jumpstart Bible Studies. Susan's desire is to equip women with the tools that help them "do life" as Jesus would. She's been married to Steve for more than 33 years and describes her grown son, Jack Bart, as "incredible."

Susan loves the heart of women, coffee, and a good story. She shares her everyday life at *www.mtyi.blogspot.com*. Stop by and say "hi" on Facebook at More Than You Imagine Ministries, or learn more about this ministry at *www.morethanyouimagine.org*.

CPSIA information can be obtained
at www.ICGtesting.com
Printed in the USA
FFHW011751220919
55112939-60822FF